Love and Liberation

Love and Liberation

By

Sharon D. Smith

ISBN 978-0-6151-4726-0

Manufactured in the United States of America

Published by Sharon D. Smith
Edited by Sharon D. Smith

First Edition

Keywords: relationships, gay marriage, homophobia, lesbians, the military

Cover design by Lulu Publishing
Back cover photography courtesy of Maxx Photography, Inc.

To submit questions, comments, or concerns about this book or for information about bulk purchase discounts, please send an email to
love_and_liberation@hotmail.com

Love and Liberation

Table of Contents

Preface

Today, we live in a world that is full of racism, terrorism, sexism, and a dozen other isms that are far too complex to understand or even mention here in a manner that would be politically correct. Many of the major television networks like CNN and FOX News, local and national newspaper headlines, and radio spotlights are always filled with breaking news stories about bloody protests and violence in the Middle East, illegal drugs in low income neighborhoods, scandalous politicians, police investigations, corporate layoffs, campus shootouts, and rising energy costs. We are also inundated with documentaries and movies about various things such as natural disasters like Hurricane Katrina, child predators, and a multitude of other pressing social, political, and economic issues.

Within all this madness, I try to find some happiness and peace within myself in order to maintain what's left of my sanity. Sometimes it works and my spirit is uplifted. I feel at ease and safe from the world. Nothing can affect me. Nothing can harm me. At other times, it doesn't work and I feel disappointed, misled, and used. I feel defenseless and unsure of what's to come. My purpose here is not to offer far-reaching solutions to the problems Americans face today or highlight what decades of politics and human nature have created. After all, I am just one person although in some cases, society would have us believe that one person's efforts can make a difference in the lives of so many people.

I just want to inform you about the joys, challenges, and struggles that are involved in many lesbian relationships. This is a book about how to deal with certain situations like infidelity, why some things happen, and what we can learn from these situations. It is a book about getting over your past, recognizing your mistakes and obligations, and being able to move forward even in the face of adversity. Although this book is written primarily for the lesbian community who struggle with their own personal relationships, it is not exclusive to lesbian relationships. There are many other women who are heterosexual, bisexual, questioning, or who have no clue how to sexually identify themselves who have gone through some of the same things presented in this book. They, too, have been hurt, mistreated, or perhaps felt neglected by the ones they love and care about. They have had questions about their own sense of self-worth and their real purpose in life. Some may have even questioned God and wondered if the things they are going through are taking place because they are being punished by God.

By writing this book, I have found a way to more effectively address the problems of my past, unresolved issues in relationships that didn't last, and learn ways in which to navigate the road that is ahead of me. It's my goal to not only entertain you, but educate you as well. In the process of entertaining and educating you, I want you to get to know me as an author and as someone who has had her fair share of ups and downs in various relationships. Understand that this book is important to me because I don't want anyone to feel they have to put up with certain things in their relationships just to be happy.

Anyone who knows me knows that I love contemporary country music. I am a true fan of great artists like Alan Jackson, Gretchen Wilson, Toby Keith, Shania Twain, and many others. Every now and then I will make an effort to lip sync every song I hear on the radio or secretly perform in my living room as if I was one of the last three anxious contestants in an American Idol or Nashville Star competition. Sometimes I pretend I am wearing a sexy black cowboy hat, snakeskin boots with a silver buckle and spurs, black Levi 501 jeans that auspiciously showcase my bowed legs, and a white, buttoned down cotton shirt like the one Bo Duke wore in the Dukes of Hazard. It is often difficult for anyone to believe that an African American can have such a fascination for this type of music when most of the music performed by African American artists is hip hop, rap, jazz, and rhythm and blues. I like to consider myself a well-rounded person who is open to just about anything.

Despite the stereotypes about country music, the truth of the matter is that much of country music focuses on issues that do not have anything to do with chugging Jack Daniels at the local saloon, saddling up horses, sleek cowboy hats, or sexy John Deere tractors. There are plenty of songs in the country music industry with themes that do not have any racial or socioeconomic boundaries such as love, liberation, and loyalty. There are songs about the love for family and friends, love found, and love lost. There are songs about being liberated from bad relationships, heartache, and other situations. There are songs about loyalty to our country, that special someone in your life, and of course, loyalty to God. It took a long time for me to recognize these underlying themes. Now, I finally see the connection between these themes and my own life through many years of good and bad experiences, as well as those experiences I wish I never had to endure.

Songs from two of my favorite country music artists, Gary Alan and Garth Brooks, have had a huge impact on me and helped focus my efforts on completing this book. Alan notes, "Life ain't always beautiful, but it's a beautiful ride." Here, the implication is that we must be prepared for whatever hand life has for us. There are good moments and bad moments. We learn to survive and move on, while learning from our mistakes. While we are going through these moments, it is important to realize that there is always a blessing in store for us. Not only that, every day that we are able to wake up and feel the sun caressing our skin is a great day.

In his song, "The Dance," Brooks proclaims "I could've missed the pain, but I'd have to miss the dance." What's interesting about Brooks' statement is the fact that we can't experience love and happiness without some level of pain and heartache. We can't experience success without being at the bottom level of the totem pole. We can't experience all the joy that life has to offer us without experiencing some of the distress it can bring. It may not always feel right or be what makes our bodies feel good, but it's all worth going through sometimes.

Together, Alan's and Brooks' verses sum up exactly how I felt for a long time, particularly in the months prior to beginning this book. I see life as a journey, an odyssey so to speak. Every day that God allows us to wake up is the start of a new adventure throughout our odyssey. In classical literature, one of the greatest odysseys ever known is Homer's *The Odyssey*, an epic tale about a brave warrior named Odysseus. Odysseus is victorious in the Trojan War and begins his ten year trip home to his wife, Penelope, in the city of Ithaca. Along the way, he encounters danger, adventure, romance, and the supernatural. When he finally arrives home, he is disguised as an old man so that he may get a better understanding of how things are without him. He quickly notices that his home is not the way he left it and that there is strife all around him.

Like Odysseus, we all have things happen to us throughout this journey we call life. There are times when we experience happiness and success. There are times when we experience pain and disappointment. We fall in and out of love. There are times when people reveal different aspects of themselves to us on a daily basis. Everyone has his or her own path to travel in life and I am no different from any of you. If you have never been in a relationship or have never been hurt by the one you pledged to spend your life with, then you may not know exactly how I feel or how anyone else feels for that matter. Again, this book is my way of moving forward. It is my way of finding liberation from all the things that have held me hostage in the past. It is also my way of reaching out to other women who may have experienced some of the same things I did.

There are so many women out there who find it difficult to understand what's going on in their personal lives in terms of their intimate relationships. And while prayer and counseling are always good remedies, sometimes you need to hear from someone who has been on the frontline of disappointment. I believe that when others can relate to and understand what you have to say, it makes things much easier and oftentimes, people will tend to learn from your mistakes as well.

This book is not necessarily an autobiography in the truest sense of the word as it also contains points of learning and mild fiction. There are some painful moments that I have trouble discussing, but to make an attempt at describing my feelings helps with my healing in so many different areas. Therefore, the events described within do not necessarily go in chronological order because life is chaotic at times and has no order. Each individual chapter in this book can be read out of order if it pleases the reader.

The names and some events in this book have been changed to protect the identity of those who had either a positive or negative impact on my life. Wherever possible, and with permission, actual names have been substituted. It is not my intention to hurt anyone's feelings or make light of anyone's unfortunate circumstances. Instead, I hope that when you read these lines, you recognize your own odyssey as it pertains to love and liberation. Enjoy.

PART I:

LOVE

*Love is the underlying motivator that provides a commitment
with strength and durability. It is the source of the energy that will keep you
honoring your commitment through all the rough spots you'll encounter...The
question is how do you know whether you are enough in love to sustain commitment?*

~Tina Tessina~
Gay Relationships

Love, the Great Goliath

Love is not a many splendid thing and whoever said so must have lived in some sort of utopia where heartache does not exist. Instead, Love is a very strange and volatile creature. She can grab hold of you and never let go. She can quickly sweep you off your feet like a tumultuous hurricane and then nonchalantly drop you on the unforgiving ground, leaving you for dead. Love can make the average person do things that she may not do under normal circumstances. Love can make you laugh and cry at the same time. On the outside, people can see your joy and happiness, but on the inside there is a typhoon of mixed emotions, disappointment, and regrets.

Love can make you believe in things that are so far removed from the truth and anything that is beneficial, that even the worse lie seems credible. Love can make you angry, bitter, or resentful. She can make you turn your back on your best friend, family members, or the one person you hold dearest to your heart. I am reminded of Julius Caesar and one of his closest companions, Brutus. Jealous of Caesar's power, Brutus conspires with other countrymen to kill Caesar. Despite the men's efforts to subdue Caesar, he tried hard to defend himself. When he saw Brutus, however, he was shocked and abruptly stopped fighting. Just before Caesar collapsed and died, he stated, "Et tu Brute" (*Julius Caesar*, III, i). Caesar could not believe that his best friend would betray him and want to kill him. Perhaps Shakespeare was on to something and recognized that even our closest friends and love ones will disappoint us for what they feel is a just cause.

Just when you think you have control of your emotions and can think rationally about anything before you, Love callously strikes you with Cupid's wicked arrow, piercing you in the deepest, most sensitive part of your entire being – your heart. Suddenly, you're back in Love's stronghold anxiously waiting for her next great move. Like an intense championship game of Chess, Love plays the queen, the most powerful piece on the board. No matter what we say or do, Love has a way of moving in any direction she chooses to capture the very things we work so hard to maintain—our pride, self-esteem, hope, and happiness. For that reason alone, we have a tendency to put up our guards and be very cautious whenever Love steps into play. There is oftentimes so much to gain when we have Love and even more to lose once Love reveals her true self.

As much as we would like to, no one can truly overcome the power of the Goliath we call Love and yet we all crave to be in her presence. We all crave to have her by our side. We all crave to bear our souls with her. We crave to have her in our lives so much that we sometimes sacrifice our own happiness and people we care about to make her love us back. Unfortunately, the universe is not designed in such a way that we can avoid Love altogether. At some point in our predetermined existence on this side of Heaven, Love will make her presence known when we say, "I love you" to someone. Regrettably, there will be only one time in our entire life that it will be a feeling that lasts forever.

Love is a very strange creature because she can also take on many forms and disguise herself as anything she wants. She can be the young lady who sits next to you at work who seems to say all the right things to arouse your ego and still be the person who is supposed to warm your bed each night. Love is also without limits. She can be cunning, cold and callous or she can be warm, witty, and wild. Even Love's worse idiosyncrasies can sometimes be justified as virtues.

In a perfect world, we want Love to be sensitive, caring, supportive, nurturing, and strong. We want her to be honest, straightforward, and have a good spirit. We want her to see past our faults, inhibitions, fears, and shortcomings. Some of us want Love to be tall, short, dark, fair, strong, have brown eyes, or any other combination of physical characteristics. Some of us are so bold that we insist that Love comes with a six-figure income, an M.B.A. or J.D. from a prestigious university like Harvard or Princeton, a 780 Beacon score, and a big suburban mansion with 20 bedrooms next to the Joneses. Maybe that's a little over the top, but there are people who desire things that are far beyond their financial and educational reach.

In essence, we want to shape Love to be what we want her to be. This is a feat that is virtually impossible to do. If it was possible, there would be no such thing as heartache or sadness and ultimately no room for betrayal, disappointment, and even regrets. The worse part is that there would be no room for personal growth and no room for learning from our mistakes. There would be no reason to ask ourselves, "Why did I stay with that person? Why didn't I see this happening before?" What in God's name was I thinking?"

As much as we would like to cultivate Love, we have to recognize that Love can't be tamed. Love is a wild animal with supernatural eyes that can see right through us and sharp claws that can tear through our very soul. Love can't be understood. Love is not a container of kids' play dough for us to shape and mold into what our imagination and our feelings want her to be. Instead, Love uses us as play dough and shapes us into the people we are now and the people we will become later.

13

Knowing what Love is and the power that Love has over a person, what does it mean to fall in love? Falling in love is what everyone dreams of. The late Gerald Levert once said, "I'd give anything, and everything to fall in love." Once during our lifetime, maybe twice, we actually fall in love with someone whom we think we will share our lives with and love even in death, as some of the greatest poets may proclaim. This is the person we share daydreams with about the way things will be when we've matured in age and wisdom and are sitting on the front porch in an antique rocking chair watching the cars pass by.

But falling in love, based on my experiences, is a myth that creates in us a "benign dementia" as Marianne Moore writes in her poem, *Love in America* (Hunter, p. 367). The mere thought of falling in love can make us crazy. We believe that falling in love has some sort of fundamental value that will make us feel good about ourselves and be the happiest we could ever be. We believe that falling in love with the right person will somehow make our lives complete. In the end, falling in love can be one of the worse things that could ever happen to anyone.

Webster's dictionary defines "fall" as to descend or tumble. It also means an overthrow or ruin. The fall of the Berlin Wall, the fall of communism in Russia, the fall of the stock market, and the fall of the Iraqi government under former dictator Suddam Hussein are all examples of things that have been overthrown or ruined. So why would we want to fall in love? Why would we want to submit ourselves or be overthrown by something that can make us cry, deceive us, or have the ability to affect every move we make? The answer is quite simple.

Despite the bad things that Love can do to us and the things she can cause us to do, we stalwartly hold on to the hope of lifelong happiness, security, and all the other things that we want Love to provide. It is this hope that keeps us wanting to have Love in our lives. It is this hope that we cling to that makes us believe in things that we truly have no way of proving their existence. We have faith that Love will not show her diabolical side, but that she will always be our trusted companion for life. We envision Love as unlike a Goliath, but rather a gentle spring breeze that we wish would last forever. We cling to the notion that our soul mate is out there somewhere waiting for us. The people we go through to get to that soul mate are just stepping stones to what we think is ultimate happiness.

Are we being deceived by Love? It's possible. Are we being naïve of the power that Love has? It's possible. Is Love the safest and most enduring emotion there is? It's unlikely. We are emotional beings endowed by God to find what makes us happy. The problem is not that we can't achieve this end. The problem is that it takes a lifetime to fully realize just what happiness really is and what it means to us.

For me, Love has been an inexhaustible cycle of regrets, disappointments, joys, and surprises. I've been in relationships where I thought the person I was with was destined to be with me forever. I've been in relationships where I was deeply in love with someone, only to realize they really meant me harm. I've been in relationships where my sweetie thought it within her rights to go beyond the boundaries of a committed relationship in order to satisfy her own inquisitiveness. In essence, Love presented herself to me as a roller coaster ride of mixed emotions and revelations. The things I've learned have been instrumental in helping me change my way of doing things and the people I choose to make a part of my life. For that reason alone, I am indebted to that great Goliath called Love. She has made me more powerful than I have ever been before simply because I know not to trust everything she represents.

Because Love can have such great power over us and all the things we do in life, it is important to be able to recognize Love in all of her mystery and wonder and change our habits accordingly. At what point do you do that? Many people ask their close friends and family members the famous question, "how do you know when you love someone?" Easy questions like these do not always have an easy answer, but there are usually enough guidelines to help us out. You will know you love someone when you can honestly read the following paragraphs and still look at your mate and say, "I love you." When it comes to knowing if you love someone, what I am about to say is not carved in any stone. They are only guidelines to help you determine if you're with someone you love or with someone you lust after.

If someone offered you a million dollars if you married her, love does not and probably would not exist in that relationship. If you are with someone simply because the sex is good and you were "lonely," love does not exist in that relationship. If you are with someone because they look good, smell good, or sound good, love does not exist there either. To love someone requires more than material things or physical attributes to make it legitimate. Love requires a strong sense of self awareness, action, and commitment.

What does self awareness have to do with love? Ask yourself these two questions. How confident are you in yourself and your abilities? Are you content with who you are and the goals you have set for yourself? If you are happy with the way you have planned your life and the things you want to accomplish, then that's a great thing. Set your sails and get started on your road to success. If you are confident in what you can do and have the skills necessary to achieve your goal, be steadfast and determined to achieve everything you want. If, at any time, you begin to doubt yourself, lose your self-esteem, or wallow in your own depression, you have forgotten what it means to love even yourself. If this is the case, you can't possibly love anyone else or have any real feelings for them outside of friendship. Instead, what will happen is that you will look for someone else to make you love and appreciate yourself rather than looking within to find where you lost your self respect and love for yourself. This ultimately leads to a false sense of security and self worth.

To love someone requires action. Unless you show people how much you care about them and love them, your words are meaningless. You may show your love for someone with flowers, candy, a quiet walk on the beach at sunset, or any other thing that makes her smile. Sometimes you have to be willing to sacrifice some things just to show your love. For example, this may mean taking one job over another to be able to spend more time with your sweetie or not associating with certain people in order to keep peace in your relationship. While these are noble acts, sometimes they can lead to problems later. When you do something because you love someone, never remind the person about it later or blame that person because of your decision to act in a certain way. If you do this, your motives are all wrong. You don't love the person you're with because you're more concerned with how will the person you're with repay you for something you did. Showing someone love is not about a tit-for-tat. It's about doing something for others because you want to, not because you're looking for a big payback.

Commitment is one of the most important aspects of love. If you love someone, you are committed to that person for as long as it is healthy to do so. You will not stray from your relationship and you will always be honest. You will work hard throughout all the rough spots in your relationship. You will talk to one another about your feelings and your desires and come up with ways to improve your relationship. If at any time you are inclined to be with someone else or if you have already stepped outside your relationship in a dishonest manner, you are no longer committed to the person you're with. You are no longer committed to working on the things that will bring you back together. You are no longer committed to loving this person. You are no longer committed to maintaining a trustworthy image of yourself.

In summary, if you know where you want to go in life and how to get there, are able to show the person you're with through your actions that you love her, and are committed to maintaining a healthy and honest relationship, then you, my friend, truly love your sweetie. Be determined to keep that love fresh and exciting. At any time, however, that you feel you are lacking in any of the three areas mentioned above, it's time to reevaluate your relationship. It's definitely time to reevaluate yourself. Don't waste your time and your sweetie's time in a relationship that might be coming to an end. Remember, Love is very powerful. That Goliath wants to control every aspect of your life, but don't let her. Learn how to first love yourself and the rest will be much easier.

Cracking the Homophobic Code

Today, we are in the midst of one of the most controversial conflicts in American history – the War in Iraq. Every day, our soldiers are losing their lives and their families are left to carry on without them. Our leaders want to ensure every American's freedom by eliminating radical groups who want to terrorize others. The greatest danger to freedom in America, however, is not the Iraqis or Islamic terrorists. The greatest threat to freedom in America is religion. Baptists, Methodists, and other religious sects are oftentimes involved in controversial debates over everything from evolution to music. Some of these people believe that children should pray while in school while others believe that literary works such as *Harry Potter* need to be banned because they promote witchcraft. Come on America! Are we so sensitive that we can't even let our children enjoy literary works that expand their creativity, imagination, and reading comprehension?

Many Americans are challenged by religious doctrines that seek to destroy or limit our freedom. One area that is particularly under attack is homosexuality and gay rights. Some people, particularly religious leaders and devout Christians, believe that being gay is a sin and an abomination. They attempt to influence legislation by using the Bible and other religious dogma as support for their viewpoints. Their agenda is based on the establishment of federal and state legislation that denies gays and lesbians the right to marry, receive death benefits and social security, obtain medical coverage and health care authority, and in most states, adopt children. The rights and privileges given to any other citizen of this country are null and void when it comes to men and women in the homosexual community.

Some people believe that there are programs, support groups, and special organizations that can deprogram you and make you heterosexual. Deprogramming, or conversion therapy as it is sometimes called, is a way of forcing someone to change their behavior, opinions, and beliefs so that they are more closely aligned with societal norms. Sometimes extreme measures are used to achieve this goal. For example, families will pay thousands of dollars for someone to use restraint, harassment, intimidation, violence, and even kidnapping to change their children and other relatives from being homosexual. Such was the case with Stephanie Reithmiller whose parents, Marita and William Reithmiller, deducted funds from their retirement account to pay $8,000 to a group of people to have their daughter kidnapped and raped repeatedly because they suspected she was being drawn into lesbianism by her college roommate (Raskin, p. 1). The only evidence Stephanie's mother had to go on was the fact that Stephanie's roommate drove a truck, oftentimes wore boots, and owned a Doberman Pinscher as a pet. In a Cincinnati court, Stephanie Reithmiller claimed that she was held against her will for seven days and on six of those nights, she was raped repeatedly. The prosecutor in this case, Simon Leis, stated, "what the parents did in the matter was done totally out of love for their daughter" (Raskin, p. 1). Unfortunately, the jury was deadlocked and all charges against the parents and the alleged kidnappers were dropped. Stephanie later pursued a civil case against her parents and the defendants for $2.75 million. The outcome of the case is unknown.

There are not too many parents out there in the world who would want their children intentionally violated, so how could the Reithmillers say they really love their daughter and that having her raped in exchange for money is a good thing? Usually, parents would be the first to demand justice for anyone who jeopardized the health and welfare of their children. It is a sad occasion when family members feel they have to resort to this type of action in order to keep their children in sync with the ways of everyone else in society. There goes individualism in America.

Some people also feel that if you decide to be gay, then you can decide not to be gay as well. When will society realize that things just don't work that way? Unlike the Staples office product commercials, there is no "Easy" button when it comes to homosexuality. By default, everything is more complicated. You lose so much of your identity when you're an out homosexual because so many other people want to dehumanize you and discriminate against you. Some even want to take your life because they may feel you are nothing more than a demon escaped from Hell who needs to quickly return. Playing the devil's advocate are all the closeted homosexuals who present themselves as being anti-gay at rallies, church functions, and so on. However, every weekend you'll see these same people in Atlanta at clubs like Bulldogs, Towers, and the Metro. You may even see them at Gay Pride events in cities like Atlanta, San Francisco, Nashville, and Washington, D.C.

Being gay is not a choice. It's not like you can snap your fingers or employ a special Clap-On, Clap-Off device and like magic, you're a respectable, God-fearing heterosexual with a husband or wife, two kids, and a cute dog. Besides, why would we choose to be something that people hate? Why would we choose to risk losing the love and support of our family and closest friends? Why would we choose to be something that people target for violence? Why would we choose to be content with the fact that the same government that we pay taxes to will treat us like third class citizens, undeserving of any of the same privileges that our neighbors receive? Why would we choose to be something that if our friends and family turned their backs on us, our only options are drugs, isolation, prostitution, or perhaps suicide? Why would we choose to be something that if we believed in the existence of Heaven and Hell, our soul would be in a never-ending inferno?

Being gay is not a choice, but rather a divine predetermined expression of one's true self whether we accept it or not. There is much evidence to support the notion that our sexual orientation is, in fact, a matter of genetic encoding. With the design of our eye color, the shape and size of our nose, and all other attributes that determine our physical existence, comes the true determination of our sexual orientation. Therefore, we're all born with an imbedded blueprint that dictates our career, our friends and family, when and how we will die, and of course, our sexual orientation.

Some people have not accepted their sexuality as their personal reality. Some people have suppressed this aspect of themselves for years and have chosen to maintain a conventional sexual identity. This is the reason there are so many closeted gays and lesbians in America today. They refuse to reveal themselves to friends and family because they are scared of rejection or maybe they have not come to terms with their sexuality. They are told they are the worse sinners and that they are going to Hell. Yet, these are the same homosexuals who choose to date and have relationships "on the down-low" and are in some of the biggest churches in the country. Rather than walk away, they continue to be battered by the teachings of their church's particular theology. They sit on the pews in silence and listen as their neighbor shouts "homosexuals are going to hell and thank God for it."

These down-low homosexuals, whether male or female, are members of Congress and the judicial system. They are teachers, police officers, doctors, lawyers, mechanics, and celebrities. They go to different gyms and play various professional sports like football or basketball. They are dedicated members of the PTA and will not hesitate to volunteer for any worthwhile fundraising event as they try to sell Krispy Kreme donuts on every block of the neighborhood. They are in all branches of the military. There are also such headliners as Bill Condon, director of *Dream Girls* and scriptwriter for the musical, *Chicago*, (Johnson, p.1) and Chris Dickerson, the first black bodybuilder to win the prestigious title of "Mr. America." It's interesting to note that Dickerson, who never admitted to being gay, was interviewed in *Genre Magazine* stating that he is "definitely not heterosexual" (Boykin, p. 1), but he has engaged in homosexual activity.

But to the Bible-toting, homophobic, and intolerant religious zealots who claim that homosexuality is a sin and an abomination, I have a few thoughts just for you. If you feel that homosexuals choose to be "that way" and can ultimately choose to be straight, at what point did you choose to be heterosexual or were you taught to be straight? If you're taught to be straight, who teaches a person to be gay? Is there a class or a new book series out there called *Homosexuality for Dummies?* If you have ever had sex before marriage, cut the corners of your beard or have a bald head, or if you have ever worn any

19

material other than linen, you, too, shall be guests in the fiery inferno. Perhaps you can explain what's going on in *The Song of Songs* of the Old Testament? If you accept one element of Leviticus as being the law, then you must accept the laws in their entirety and not stray from them. Choosing one line of scripture while ignoring the rest is unfair.

If it is wrong to take another man's life, according to scripture, why is there not a push by religious leaders to stop the type of violence that ended the life of young Matthew Sheppard, a 21-year old University of Wyoming student who was brutally beaten, tortured, and left tied to a fence to die? Rather than mourn the loss of a young student with a promising future, one religious leader touted Sheppard's death as a well-deserved punishment. In 1998, Fred Phelps of the Westboro Baptist Church showed up at Sheppard's funeral displaying signs that read "No Fags in Heaven" and "God Hates Fags." In the midst of the wars in Iraq and Afghanistan, Phelps even applauds the deaths of U.S. soldiers because he believes they represent this nation's tolerance of homosexuality. According to Phelps, any soldier's death is punishment for their sin of tolerance (Fred Phelps and the Westboro Church…).

Violence against anyone based on a person's differences is wrong. A person's sexuality should not be justification for treating her unjustly, abusing her, or in any other manner violating her personal space. Disrespecting a grieving family during a funeral is even more heinous. This is not to say that all religious groups subscribe to Phelps' teachings or his church, but when have you seen one of the mainstream churches picket the hazing, violence, and blatant discrimination of homosexuals that occurs across the nation, particularly in the African American community? I am yet to be a witness to that occasion. Perhaps we should ask some of the Dollars, Longs, and Jakes of the world for their opinion on this matter. In his book, *Man in the Middle,* former NBA star John Amaechi talks about his career in the NBA with the Utah Jazz, the Cleveland Cavaliers, the Orlando Magic, and several other professional teams. He also talks about his decision to reveal to the world that he is gay. In reference to Matthew Sheppard, Amaechi states, "I adore it [this country] on many levels, but we live in a country where a shoeless child can be strapped to a fence post and left to die…And yet somehow we expect that the general public will sit up and pay attention" (Amaechi Says…, p. 1).

If homosexual relationships destroy the framework of traditional family values, what do you have to say about homosexual relationships that last ten, twenty, or more years? Which one of your family's values is being compromised by two, consenting same-sex adults who are attracted to one another and who want to be in an intimate relationship with one another? Where is the respect for family values and the bonds of marriage when celebrities get engaged and then divorce after being married six months or less? What about the homosexual couple who raises a child together and gives it all the love and support possible and the child ends up as one of the top business leaders in the country? My guess is that homosexuals have to try harder than others because of the inherent discrimination in the workplace, government, and other organizations.

I once heard a popular nationally syndicated radio talk show host, Neal Boortz, question a listener who called the show to discuss "what the Bible says" about homosexuality. The caller was quick to focus on Mosaic laws, how the Bible was written for Jews, and that scripture says homosexuality is wrong. Boortz quickly responded by asking the caller how can he be sure what is right and wrong and what is a sin when it comes to homosexuality if the scriptures that the caller quoted were written by men thousands of years earlier and translated many times since then. He went on to ask the caller how he can say that homosexuality is such a bad thing if Jesus never talked about the subject. The caller stated that some people may say that Jesus never talked about rape either, but that doesn't make it right. While this may be true, rape is an attack against one's right to not be subjected to unwanted physical contact. Homosexuality is a matter of attraction to one gender versus another.

Sex among consenting adults, no matter what their sexual orientation, is not wrong. Someone should have said this to Senator Rick Santorum who feels it is fine to be homosexual as long as you are not having homosexual sex. In a 2003 interview with the Associated Press, Santorum stated that homosexual acts are somehow threats to society and the family. He compared homosexuality to bigamy, incest, and adultery. Where in the world does he get this? This is one of the guys elected to represent America?

In his book, *Somebody's Gotta Say It,* Boortz states that the problem has nothing to do with homosexuality, but rather the problem lies with the people who constantly promote their hate-filled, homophobic ideologies. Boortz has long stated his opinion that some religious fanatics are so obsessed with hating someone who is different than they are and try to push their agendas in the public arena such as the state and federal government and make efforts to amend the U.S. Constitution to deny certain citizens their right to life, liberty, and the pursuit of happiness. Needless to say, Boortz's viewpoints oftentimes breed complaints from some of his listeners. People across the nation try to have his show banned.

I don't want to get into a religious debate and I do not want to offend any of my astute readers. I am not so naïve as to believe that all religious leaders and Christians share the same hate-filled opinions. There are, although few in number, some people who truly believe that God sees not our sexual orientation, but our devotion to Him. I know God for myself and only I know the wonderful things He has done for me and I will share some of those things later in this book. However, it is not for you to judge me or anyone else; you are commanded to love your neighbors, not hate them for who they are.

Not only is there a push to deprogram homosexuals, some people believed they are equipped with special powers. I find it very humorous that some people think they know what being gay looks like. If they see a woman with a short, natural haircut like mine, she's automatically gay. If they see a man with a pink shirt, then they assume he is gay or has "gay tendencies."

Sometimes all it takes is for people to conclude a woman is gay is for her to drive a big truck, not wear make-up, be athletic or enjoy sports, or perhaps wear jeans all the time. These things do not determine a person's sexuality. What a person drives or the activities they're involved in is a matter of choice. Being gay doesn't have a certain look or style or voice that can be easily recognized 100% of the time. It just is.

I have never heard of anything as ignorant as people saying "they can change" a person and make him or her straight again. The nerve of some people to be so confident in themselves that they think their love-making ability is the much anticipated cure to homosexuality in America. I laugh at them. Their claims should be patented, packaged in an air tight plastic container, and added to the Black Kow line of compost products with the phrase, "Maximum Strength Fertilizer." I bet this would make the people at Home Depot and Lowe's happy. Who knows. Maybe these same people who have this uncanny ability to convert homosexuals are just curious to know if they "still got it" and what actually goes on behind closed doors. Perhaps this is a topic for another book altogether.

What is even more interesting is the military's stance on gays and lesbians who voluntarily defend this country on a daily basis against every type of enemy imaginable. Even now, there are hundreds of gays and lesbians stationed in various parts of the world who vowed to sacrifice their own lives so that we civilians can enjoy every freedom guaranteed by the laws of this country and our great Constitution. The "don't ask, don't tell" policy has its benefits and consequences. No one is required to admit their sexuality, but if they do, they are effectively relieved of duty. A service member may or may not be honorably discharged for revealing their sexual orientation. Apparently, some military leaders feel only heterosexual service members are capable of pulling a trigger during combat and representing this country in the manner in which it should be represented. If Osama Bin Laden was about to shoot me and the only person that could save me was a little butch of a woman with a deep voice and a great aim, then I say go for it. Shoot that crazy bastard and let's go have a Heineken or some Patron because I probably just wet my pants from being in total fear.

Before I go on, I must set the record straight. I respect and admire everyone in the armed services. They make sacrifices that most of us are not willing to make for total strangers. For that, I am grateful for their hard work and their commitment to protecting U.S. citizens wherever they may be. It is our government, however, that I am worried about. Our government, backed by Christian lobbyists and conservative homophobes, places its anti-gay stance above the safety and security of this nation. In the midst of the War in Iraq, members of the Bush Administration admit there is a huge deficit in the number of translators in the military, particularly those trained in Arabic and Farci. These are two of the languages that terrorists use to communicate with one another. However, more than 300 trained language specialists have been discharged from the military because of its "don't ask, don't tell" policy, including 50 who were trained in Arabic. In a recent article in *The Washington Post*, Alan Simpson questions these service members' dismissal by stating, "Is there a 'straight' way to translate Arabic? Is there a 'gay' Farci?" (Simpson, A15).

I do not understand how a person's sexuality would hinder his or her job performance, combat readiness, or negate his oath to serve this country. There are thousands of homosexual veterans in the U.S., some of whom have been seriously injured or maimed in the line of duty. Other homosexual service members have even been killed in the line of duty. Yet, they all have served, and are still serving, our country in silence. The Servicemembers Legal Defense Network, a gay rights advocacy group, believes that nearly 65,000 troops are currently serving in the military by hiding their sexual orientation (Means, p. 1). The group further reports that since the implementation of Bill Clinton's "don't ask, don't tell" policy, "more than 11,000 soldiers have been dismissed for having their private lives exposed" (Means, p. 1). And our country wants to take away their basic freedoms and deny them the same rights as others? This is not one of the things that make this country the best place in the world to be. It is one of the things that give gratification to our enemies knowing that our country's leaders are more concerned with what goes on in its citizens' homes rather than promoting national security. Military leaders should be more concerned with a soldier's conduct and bravery rather than who that soldier is dating.

Our nation's leaders would rather spend time getting two-thirds vote in the House and Senate to add a U.S. Constitutional amendment that defines marriage between one man and one woman. An even bigger slap in the face of homosexuals is how our government is trying to make it easier for criminal aliens in this country to get health coverage, free education, and absolutely no or limited tax liability. The people who helped build this country, fund its programs, and defend it are being ostracized by the government they are forced to support and lobbyists whose sole purpose is to legitimize heterosexuality while criminalizing homosexuality. Instead of the government focusing its efforts on dehumanizing homosexuals, why doesn't it concentrate on such things as passing the Fair Tax, which will allow Americans the opportunity to keep more of their hard earned money rather than paying high income taxes to fund politicians' pork barrel projects. Perhaps the government can be more active at protecting our borders. There are so many more pressing matters in this country.

Let's face it. There is such a huge burden upon the homosexual community to behave, think, and perform according to society's definition of normal. For example, it is more customary, and acceptable, for two people of the opposite sex to be involved in a relationship or have sexual intercourse. Anyone who is involved in a homosexual relationship can not possibly love one another and, therefore, could not possibly want to have children and raise a family of their own. Therefore, homosexuals are considered to be "anti-family." While it is true that children need to have parental involvement in their lives, there is no set of rules that stipulate the parents must be married and of the opposite sex. Again, society is relying on its religious beliefs to say what individuals can and can not do in the privacy of their own homes. I am anxiously waiting for the day when religion is not the basis for laws in this country. Perhaps I'm dreaming too much.

U.C.L.A. Kid

I grew up as a lesbian in Atlanta, Georgia. In fact, my entire childhood and young adult years prepared me for the moment I would tell my friends, people in my family, and coworkers that the person they thought they knew really was just a façade of someone who was desperately trying to find a comfortable hiding place. As early as five years old, I knew there was something singular about me. I knew I didn't fit in perfectly with the way everyone else around me was thinking. I thought it was strange for me to look at pictures in different magazines and feel a level of excitement that paralleled the way my male cousins felt. I thought it was strange for me to be in a relationship with a guy, a member of the high school football team, for more than six months and not ever have the desire to kiss him. I thought it was strange for me to feel attracted to other girls when I didn't see anyone else around me exhibiting the same type of attraction.

I recall looking at the girls in my classroom and wondering how I could kiss them on the cheek without getting slapped or getting caught by my teachers. Beginning as early as the fourth grade, I realized I had a huge crush on a certain group of girls in my class. There was just something about their smile and how they dressed. There was something in how they pulled out their glittery lip balm and gracefully applied it. More than anything, I liked their inability to deal with bugs and mean boys on the playground because there I was to save the day. Of course I never said anything and I didn't do anything to reveal my little secret crushes. I wasn't sure why that was the best thing to do at the time, but I didn't. Growing up, I never knew I was a U.C.L.A. kid – an undercover lesbian in Atlanta. For that matter, I never knew I would be writing a book twenty-five years later about my experiences.

My mother may not recall this moment, but she and I were sitting in the kitchen one day talking about every day things. Suddenly, she just came out and asked me, "Are you a lesbian?" I was only about ten years old and I didn't know what that big word meant. For a ten year old, that was a big question for a little person. She said that a lesbian is a girl who likes another girl the same way a girl would like a boy. Then she broke it down for me again just to make

25

sure I understand the question. A lesbian, she said, is a girl who wants a girlfriend and not a boyfriend. "That's not you, is it?" After this explanation, I emphatically said, "no way, Mama!" The manner in which she asked and the tone of her voice suggested I should say something to ease her mind. A negative answer was all I could come up with. It was then that I discovered there was a name for this strange attraction I had for girls and that I was essentially a lesbian. I just didn't know what to do with my new found knowledge or how to proceed from that point on. So, I just kept my feelings to myself for years and years. And while I didn't come out of the closet that day, it was probably the moment I realized there was a 40-watt bulb that had been flickering on and off for years and somebody needed to do something about it. That's usually a sign of something big.

During my adolescent stage, I tried to keep my focus on one particular boy in my class who I thought was cute and so did everyone else. There was one time when our class was having an election to choose a class leader. Just like some of today's political candidates, his campaign was very persuasive. He asked for the girls to vote for him and in exchange he would show a certain part of his anatomy. Let's just say his slogan was "Ring-a-Ling, Vote for Me and I'll Show You My Ding-a-Ling." Wow. That didn't work on me and it still doesn't. I wanted the shiny black and red Hot Wheels cars with the white racing stripes that he offered the boys in exchange for their votes. I don't remember who won that election, but I hope this young man didn't run for any public office with that same slogan. Then again, for some political candidates, this may be the only thing that may get them into office.

In our neighborhood, there was a candy lady. She sold everything from grape sodas and potato chips to bubble gum and licorice. I remember stopping by her house from time to time on my way to school. A pocket full of change went a long way back then. I had about $1.75 each day and I was on a mission to sweep some girl off her feet with all the chocolate and gooey stuff I could possibly buy. I would stock up on one cent bubble gum, Lemon Heads, Johnny Appleseeds, Tootsie Rolls, and Jaw Breakers. When I got to school, I would share my bubble gum and Now and Laters with certain girls and I would sell that same gum and candy to the boys for a nickel each. That allowed me to buy more candy. I was an entrepreneur at an early age. I didn't have a problem giving away my goodies to the young cuties. That kept them coming back to me, their personal sugar mama, even if they didn't know that I had ulterior motives.

I suppose at that time I was a stud in training, always looking to make the girls smile, do nice things for them, carry their books, and so on. Little did I know I had formulated what type of girl I liked long before I even knew what was meant by fem, aggressive fem, stud, lipstick lesbian, butch, soft stud, and versatile. I was a huge tomboy who loved playing kickball, dodge ball, and flag football. The other girls just wanted to play on the swings, gossip, or jump rope. I was a rebel. I didn't see any fun in jumping on squares numbered 1 through 10 and picking up a small stone as if I had conquered the universe in one giant leap. I didn't see any fun in comparing one person's purse contents with someone else's and there definitely wasn't any fun in playing Jacks. But the girls who did these things were incredibly cute to me. That's when physical education was fun. Back then, the girls didn't wear these high rise pants or skirts that were so short they looked like clothing for a Barbie Doll. I'm all about a person being fashionable, but there has to be a cut-off point somewhere.

Physical education class was fun, but I was actually one of the few kids who really enjoyed school. I was one of the smartest kids in my class and I always received some sort of award for something – Citizen of the Year, Perfect Attendance, Star Student, Principal's List, Honor Roll, and so on. However, that didn't stop me from being what some may call the class clown. I would do just about anything to get the girls I had secret crushes on to laugh. Most times it worked. At other times, I would hear a loud voice yelling in the background, "Sharon Smith, calm down or you'll stand in the corner." Anytime a grownup used your full name, it was never a good sign. The words that teacher blasted out at me were powerful because that corner would inevitably lead to a one-on-one conference between my behind and rawhide on the home front. If you grew up in the south and had parents and relatives like mine, then there was always the possibility of rawhide being substituted with a switch.

In the sixth grade, I narrowed my crush down to just one single girl. We spent a lot of time together. To me, she was my secret girlfriend. I'm sure to her I was just someone who had a lot of candy and knew how to spell all the hard words like "poisonous" on those easy spelling tests. I have seen her only a few times in the past five years or so. After high school, she went to college in one of the Carolinas. I saw her a few times when I worked Downtown. The last time I saw her, she was working at a local bank. We exchanged phone numbers and small talk, but that was about it. I wanted to tell her that I was her secret admirer for a number of years, but I didn't. If I ever see her again, I won't waste the opportunity to spill the beans.

For some people, and I'm no different, the high school years are the most challenging period in a person's life. It's the time we develop lasting friendships, and in some cases, solidify personal relationships with people we are greatly fond of. It is a time when self image is very important. How we dress, the people we date, the places we go, and how we talk to one another are all factors in how we identify ourselves and how we choose to interact with others. For me, high school was fun, but it was also hard for me to keep this attraction I had for girls to myself.

I was forced to keep my sexual identity to myself. I couldn't talk to anyone. I retreated to doing what I did best – be a nerd and play basketball. Nowadays, many people feel that if you're a girl and you play high school basketball, or any sport, you're a lesbian anyway. That wasn't the case for many of my teammates. The conversations we had in the locker room were not unlike most locker room conversations. They talked about guys. They talked about the game. They talked about the fans. For the most part, I was quiet.

27

There was nothing I could say. There were so many people in school who thought that I was gay, even though I did nothing to bring them to that conclusion. After all, I had a boyfriend. Today, I realize that having a boyfriend means absolutely nothing at all.

What amazes me about some of the people I went to high school with and who accused me of being gay are some of the same people I saw years later at gay clubs, bookstores, and other social functions with their girlfriends. So you see, it's hard keeping a part of you a secret. You tend to go through extreme measures just to protect your identity. That's sad and I know this first hand. I once heard an acquaintance of mine say that it was important for her to tell her family about her sexual orientation. It wasn't that she wanted to cause trouble or anything like that. Her logic was based on a simple question. She asked, "what will people write on my tombstone?" She went on to say that she didn't want anyone to speak of her life in a manner in which she did not live. I couldn't agree with her more. When I die, I want people to say that I was true to my own beliefs, that I never backed down from a good debate, and that the people who knew me could truly call me a friend. That is what I want people to say about me. The rest is irrelevant.

Someone Hit the Switch

The spring of 1994 completely changed my life and started me on my way to realizing that I was more attracted to women than I ever will be toward men. It was also the point I began to accept myself for being the way I am. I could focus on the rest of the world's acceptance one person at a time.

It was in 1994 that I first kissed a girl. It took me by surprise. She worked as a store manager at a retail store in the mall. I worked as a cashier in the food court. She would come to my restaurant every day, smiling with the cutest little dimples just dancing off her cheeks. She ordered the same thing each time – a gyro combo, no salt on the fries, and an extra large Dr. Pepper with light ice. We exchanged small talk about the weather, college, basketball, and other little things. What really connected us to one another and started our friendship was hair.

We've all experienced bad hair days. When she approached me I was having a bad hair week so my Mercer University baseball cap was the perfect cover up. I was the ponytail queen in my black and orange fitted cap for that entire week. One day she came to the restaurant and ordered her usual meal. Out of nowhere, she just came out and said to me, "you look very cute in a hat" and then like a western outlaw, she walked away. My eyes followed her from the counter and through the maze of people, tables, and chairs in the food court. I thought to myself, "What is she talking about?" I was obviously riding on the short bus at just the thought that someone complimented me in such a way, particularly another girl. Why would she tell me I was cute? Did she pick up on some kind of vibe that I was unaware I even had? What were her intentions? What would I say when, and if, she came back? I didn't know what gaydar meant then, but I guess hers went crazy whenever she was near me.

The rest of the day went by very quickly. I couldn't help thinking about this young, attractive woman who actually flirted with me. Unfortunately, there was no one I could tell about my exhilarating experience. For all I knew, this little secret would follow me to my grave. I couldn't think of anyone to ask for advice so I just spent the rest of the day smiling and saying to myself that baseball cap would be my best friend for a few more days.

A few days later, she offered to give me a ride home. I didn't think it might not be a good idea to get in a car with a total stranger, but I did. After all, she was cute and had a beautiful smile. I didn't see anything wrong with it. When we got to my house, we said hello to my mother, and went into my room. My mother was standing in the kitchen. I introduced her to my new friend and we casually walked to my room. Just as I was showing her my collection of Tweety and Elmo dolls, she moved closer to me and kissed me. Initially, I had that deer caught in the headlights look. I felt I was on Candid Camera or that I had been punked by Ashton Kutcher. Her lips were so soft and I could tell she had recently coated them with some sort of fruity lip gloss, perhaps strawberry or cherry. Her sweet, dainty perfume permeated my room. I didn't want her to leave, but I would have had a hard time explaining to my mother why I had an overnight guest all of a sudden. Maybe she would think something strange and maybe she wouldn't. I wasn't ready to take the chance and I didn't want to have that lesbian conversation again.

We spent some more time together after that and talked on the phone a lot. There was never anything serious because she already had a girlfriend. Unfortunately, she said she wasn't completely happy in that relationship. I tried to talk her into walking away from that relationship, but she either couldn't or wouldn't. I guess she loved this crazy person too much to step away. I tried to assure her that she shouldn't have to go through some of the things she discussed with me, but my efforts were in vain. I just wanted her to be happy.

One of the things we liked doing for each other was making mixed tapes of various artists like Prince, Freddie Jackson, Keith Sweat, and others. Her favorite song was Tevin Campbell's Brown Eyed Girl. I liked that song, too, because she had the most beautiful, big, brown eyes I had ever seen and a smile that would make even the stars jealous. Her voice was soft, but slightly raspy. It was inviting. Eventually we lost touch with each other, but I saw her again at a novelty store about three years later. She said she was doing well. I haven't seen her since then, but I hope that wherever she is, she's happy.

I was introduced to my first real girlfriend about two months later. In just a short amount of time, I discovered the world of lesbian role-playing. I learned that I didn't like whatever role she was playing. I was uncomfortable with whatever role she put me in as well, or it could have been just the way things worked out. Either way, I wasn't interested in it and it didn't excite me. She wasn't dainty like the girls I encountered in grade school. She didn't have her nails done or a cute, sophisticated hairstyle. She was loud and boisterous. She dressed like a guy, but her voice sounded like a hurt mouse that just got caught in a trap, lured in by the strong smell of cheddar cheese. I guess you could say she was a stud. I suppose that at the time, that didn't matter to me. She was my first female relationship.

Ever since my first kiss, I was ready for my first intimate encounter. I wondered what it would be like. Would it be better than being with a guy?

Would it be worse? Would I change up all together and go back to dating guys because the intimate experience was nothing like I anticipated? Would it hurt? How do two women have sex? Are there any special rules I have to follow? These are all questions I never got answers to prior to meeting her for a number of reasons. I never saw any videos of women having sex so I didn't know what it would be like. I never saw a woman naked other than the ones in Playboy magazine. There was no one I could talk to about this whole thing either.

I can't say that my first time was anything special. I didn't know what to expect. It happened in the early morning hours around 2:00 AM. It was late and I was tired, but she made the first move and I, obviously nervous, curious, and anxious at the same time, let her. She could tell I was nervous and insisted that I relax. She kissed me on my neck and chest then proceeded to rub my breasts. Before I knew it, she had unbuttoned my shirt, released my bra, and my head rested comfortably on the two pillows on my bed. She kissed my navel and then slowly went further south. I knew what was about to happen, but at the same time, I didn't know what to expect. Until that point, I hadn't even seen any pornographic or Playboy versions of what sex among women should look like. I ached with anticipation. What's next? Will this be as good as it was during my intimate moments with guys? The wait was over. Five minutes later, so was she. I guess it does take three licks to get to the center of a tootsie pop. Either that or I became an expert at faking the good stuff because the experience was not what I expected.

I thought to myself, "Is this all I get? What just happened? Are you tired? Did I do something wrong?" I was disappointed to no end. What happened to the foreplay? What about holding me when this whole fiasco was over? Time was not an issue, but rather my level of satisfaction was at negative 100. She definitely didn't make me feel comfortable about having sex with other women, but I soon found satisfaction—just not with her.

After years of hiding out in the safety and security of the proverbial closet and being in a relationship with my second girlfriend, I finally took a peak outside the door and jumped out. The first person I told was my best friend, Troy. He didn't believe me, but he had to accept it. My brother was next in line. It was a few months later that I actually told him. His response was simply "and…" as if he was waiting for me to complete my thoughts. He then said that as long as I was happy, he was cool with whatever I wanted. Telling my brother was easy. Even now, he and I talk about a wide variety of things. We share stories about who we think is gay in Hollywood, sex, and so on. From time to time, he and I have even shared moments when we would go girl-gazing together. His tastes in women are definitely unlike mine. He liked big boobs and big behinds. I liked long, sexy legs and a pretty smile.

I was terrified when I told my mother I was gay. I would have rather jumped from a burning building a million stories high than tell my mother that her dream of her little girl walking down the aisle in a long wedding dress standing next to Denzel Washington, or at least someone who was just as sexy, was not going to come to pass. However, it was forced upon me to tell her this

31

simple, yet haunting secret. Fear and anxiety took over my entire body. To say I was terrified was an understatement. But, after getting caught hugging my girlfriend at the time, it was time to confess or be in the strange situation of having to start a conversation with "see, Mama, what had happened was…" I was certain she would kick me out of the house. I only had $14.58 and a peppermint in my pocket, not enough for the Greyhound bus or even the sleaziest hotel room so I could hide out and gather my thoughts.

It is never easy to tell your family that you're gay. Sometimes the reaction is not what you expect. Sometimes there is just long silence or strange looks. Sometimes the words are just too hard to say and you end up standing in silence once again. With me, my mother's questions were thrown at me left and right. Why do you want to be with women? Don't you know it's not safe? What about all the boyfriends you've had? Where did you learn this behavior? Why do you want to have sex with women? I can't fault her, or any other parent in the world for asking these questions. It's natural. They feel something was overlooked during your childhood or perhaps someone was negatively influencing you. But, after a few hours of assuring her that there was nothing wrong with my upbringing, that she did nothing wrong to influence my sexuality, and that my feelings for girls were there since kindergarten, she stated the same thing my brother did. It took a few more years for us to really be able to talk candidly about homosexuality and what homosexuals go through in terms of violence, politics, and other important areas. For me, this is the greatest part of our relationship.

In late 1997, the last person to find out about my sexuality was my father. For some strange reason, I was nervous. At the same time, I felt he could accept it or not and it wouldn't bother me one bit. Our relationship wasn't the most perfect one in the world as we didn't see eye to eye on a lot of things. I oftentimes felt neglected because when I needed him, he rarely came through for me. I sensed I was toward the lower end of his list of priorities. I never mentioned this to him. I was hoping he would just know.

For no reason at all, I just wanted to call him to say hello and see how he was doing. We exchanged pleasantries and then I said to him, "I'm gay." There was no hesitation or forethought in my statement. I just said it. Ready to engage in conflict, I waited for his response. He simply said that as long as I was happy, he was, too. I never heard him speak like that before. I was surprised and relieved. In 1999, he was found dead in his home from a gunshot wound to the head. Whether it was suicide or murder is still a mystery to me. I sometimes think about him and wish things could have been better between us. I can only hope that, wherever he is now, he knows that I miss him.

I don't suggest to any of you to come out to your family if you haven't already done so. It's not an easy thing to do. In fact, it can be the hardest task you'll ever have to face. Some people prefer to keep the security of their happy homosexual home and be on the down-low at the same time. This works for some people. But you have to be honest with yourself and others. What really makes you happy? Are you comfortable keeping a part of you hidden from your family? Is it more convenient for you to maintain this secret? Whatever motivates you, just be true to yourself.

The New Car Phase

We all want to be in healthy, happy relationships. We want to be with someone who will treat us with respect and will not lie to us. We want to have someone in our lives to go to the movies with or attend a family reunion. We want to cuddle up with someone special, have some popcorn, and share some of our deepest secrets. We want to laugh at one another's silly jokes. We want to be able to tell our friends and loved ones how we totally screwed up our first Thanksgiving dinner by burning the turkey to a royal crisp. We want to go on vacations together, arcades, and anywhere else in the world that would be fun and romantic. These are the good times, the calm before the storm. Some people call it the honeymoon phase of a relationship, but I like to call it the new car phase.

The new car phase is very similar to the honeymoon phase of a relationship. Just in case some of you are far removed from the honeymoon phase or have never really experienced it, let me briefly explain this phenomenon. The honeymoon phase begins when we make a conscience decision to be with someone in a monogamous relationship. We have committed ourselves to being with this person for as long as it is healthy to do so. When we initially enter a relationship with someone, everything is brand new. We call each other weird names like Pooky-Bear or Tater Tot. Even if her jokes are nowhere near funny, we laugh anyway. We gaze into each other's eyes as if there is some secret code written on each other's iris that will give us the answer to the famous question, "what is the meaning of life?" Every sentence ends with a "yes, dear" or "what would you like to do, Honey?" We make ourselves look and sound like fools just to please our mate and get her to laugh. During the honeymoon phase, even sex is better. We are willing to try anything and try it anywhere. There are no boundaries. We essentially act like the Energizer Bunny when it comes to sex – all day, every day; we are ready to get our groove on. Yes, everything is great during the honeymoon phase.

Contrary to the honeymoon phase, the new car phase can have a shorter lifespan and be more intense. For example, when we get a new car, we are careful about where we park so as not to be too close to the idiots who have to swing their door wide open and dent our vehicle with their door. We take the time to wash the car every Saturday afternoon, a process which may take at least three hours. We wash, rinse, wash, and rinse again. Even if just one mosquito or other flying insect lands on the windshield, the whole process starts again. The tires get the best Armor All shine. The dash gets the royal cleaning treatment. No one is allowed to eat, drink, or smoke in the car. You get the oil changed every 3,000 miles and regular maintenance is conducted at exactly the recommended mileage. The fuel tank is always full with quality gasoline from only one, well-known gas station. The interior is always clean, vacuumed, and smells like the car just left the manufacturer and went straight to your house. We instantly choose a name to fit the car's "personality" and we may even go as far as to get personalized license plates. So now, your new car's name is Rough Rider with a license plate that reads "RUARIDR."

After a few months, the new car smell goes away and is replaced with the scent of Fritos and Dr. Pepper. Mickey D fries have fallen into the abyss underneath the driver's seat. The cup holders are now filled with pennies and empty gum wrappers. In no time at all, RUARIDR changes its call sign to DUSTY. You take the car to the local car wash during lunch for a $9.99 interior vacuum and exterior wash—no need to wait for it to dry; you're on a mission to get going somewhere very important. You realize you dented your own door pulling into the Shell station by banging it on the pole that sits just before the fuel dispensers. But, that's no big deal to you right now. You rush in to get the cheapest gas possible wherever that may be. When you've reached the end of the new car phase, it's clear to everyone around you including your friends and family. You've changed how you take care of the things you value.

In relationships, reality kicks in and reminds you that your new car phase is just about over. It's now time to put it in reverse and actually look at what's happening in your relationship and learn about your mate's little idiosyncrasies. Perhaps the fact that she leaves a cup on the counter really upsets you. Perhaps you don't like the fact that she wants you to cook all the time. Perhaps she annoys you when you're watching television and she calls your name for no reason at all. When the new car phase is over, your little Pooky-Bear turns into a Grizzly Bear. It happens to all of us.

In one of my relationships, the new car phase ended, but the young lady I was involved with didn't see things that way. She thought that everything was supposed to be the same as they were in the beginning of our relationship. She thought I should have kept writing little notes and saying little cute things to make her feel special. That's just fine. If you start out doing those things, you should keep doing them. At the same time, we must realize that people change and our viewpoints of each other start to change as well. For example, after a period of time, I began seeing this young lady as being over-sensitive, moody, and a real challenge to be around sometimes. She, on the other hand, didn't see things that way and began to view me as being complacent and insensitive. There were other issues that plagued our relationship. The end result was a rapid plunge into chaos and misunderstandings. Our relationship went from being the equivalent of the Lexus LS 460 HL that parks itself to an old Yugo that was obsolete, uneventful, and too confined. I went from happy to fed up in a matter of months. Like a car, I wish that relationship came with a warranty or at least some type of disclaimer to let me know what types of problems to look out for. Then again, when people are trying to sell you a lemon, they're not going to tell you about its weaknesses.

We all know that troubles will come and that the relationship will be tested several times. Sometimes the relationship will be tested to the point where you're just not sure if you should stay or walk away. You wonder if it's all worth it. You start saying to yourself, "do I really want to put up with her" or "she never does this or that." In one of my last relationships, I realized the new car phase was over and it was time to figure out what to do for the rest of our time together. Unfortunately, she didn't see things that way.

Your relationship will not always be about the things you used to do. Sometimes each of your personalities gets in the way of keeping things the way they used to be. Sometimes people move forward in their relationship too fast for it to develop and be nurtured properly. I'm sure we've all heard the popular scenario where people will go on three dates and then the fourth date is all about planning from which location the U-Haul truck will be rented. When any of these things happen, be careful. Don't set yourself up for a quick end to your relationship. Take your time and watch it grow.

While the new car phase can be fun, it can also be an opportunity for you to gather your thoughts and try to see things for what they really are on the surface. For example, in time, you may see that your sweetheart wasn't meant for you, just as you might discover that Rough Rider may have been too much for you to handle. There may have been a time when the two of you were able to talk to one another about everything from syrup and hotcakes to deeply kept secrets about your past. Towards the end of the new car phase, every conversation may seem forced because of certain insecurities, self-esteem problems, finances, and so on.

However, the real trouble does not start in a relationship until someone mentions those three little words—"I love you." At that point, you're stuck in the relationship. You have to put forth more effort to make things work because it's not just you and your mate anymore. It's you, your mate, and each other's feelings that make the relationship more difficult to maneuver. When you say, "I love you" to someone, you have to mean it and you have to feel it. Love is more powerful than you think. So, while you're enjoying the new car phase, know that changes will come at some point in your relationship. You must be prepared for what may happen later down the line. You have to decide if you're going to stick with that old car until every nut and bolt falls off because it has been good to you in the past and has gotten you through life. If you don't keep it, what car will be more to your liking and provide you with the same quality and loyalty? In other words, will you stick with the same person until you've both matured in age and work out your problems or will you take a chance on someone who may not be just perfect for you and may not provide you with the same loyalty and commitment that you're accustomed to?

Whatever choice you make in terms of your relationship, be sure that you're honest with the person you're involved with. It's not fair to anyone to be in the dark about situations that concern both parties in the relationship. So, when you've recognized the fact that your relationship has neared the end of its new car phase, try, if feasible, to salvage what's left of the relationship. You may not need a total overhaul or a trade-in. Sometimes all it takes is a minor tune up to get things going in the right direction again.

Thank God for
Friends and Family

Love comes in many shapes and sizes and colors. She greets us right where we are in life and proceeds with the process of changing us in some kind of way. Throughout that process of change, we tend to rely heavily on our closest friends and family members for guidance and support. No matter where we are in life or what our day to day activities may be, we must recognize that friends and family are important. And while we may not like everyone in our family, we certainly have an obligation to love them. As far as our friends go, there are only a select few that can touch our lives in a uniquely positive manner.

I only have a select group of friends that I am comfortable hanging out with or sharing ideas. One of my best friends is Troy. Whenever Troy and I hang out, you can bet the house we're at a nearby Starbucks having a tall latte and surfing the internet or having lunch at a local café. Unfortunately, it would usually be at my expense. Next to me, Troy is one of the biggest tight-wads in America. Because of that, we always look at each other and one of the first things we say to one another is, "who's paying?"

Troy and I talk about just about anything including sex, religion, and politics. I've known him since middle school, about twenty years now. What started out as his way of showing interest in me by chasing me around the room in algebra class blossomed into a great friendship. He has a certain way of getting under your skin with some of the things he says. He spends much of the time talking about quantum physics or some other boring topic like engineering or mathematics. Somehow he taught himself a lot about architecture, real estate, and other disciplines. Without having completed all four years of college, he has amassed enough knowledge and experience to teach even the smartest students at schools like Georgia Tech or MIT. I sometimes get to the point where I have to just say, "Troy, your speaking privileges have been temporarily revoked. Any further utterances will result in castration of the tongue." Overall, he is a nice guy and I love him dearly.

38

My other best friend is Anjeannette, or simply Angie. We met in high school and eventually discovered we had a lot of things in common. She was my road dog, my buddy, and my partner in crime. We shared so many secrets and oftentimes laughed at some of the crazy things we used to do. I recall one day we went to a Mexican restaurant near Lindberg Station and had about twelve margaritas – peach and strawberry were our weapons of choice. From there, we thought we were true warriors as we decided to go bowling. I quickly discovered that when you have a buzz from alcohol, holding a bowling ball is an extremely difficult task. For some reason, the weight of the ball causes you to lose your balance and travel down the bowling lane along with it on its journey to make a strike. The ball finally released itself from my hand. I rolled a 7-10 split in that frame. We were definitely off our rockers that day, but we had fun. Unfortunately, Angie moved to Germany with her husband, Travis, who is stationed in the Army. I missed being able to pick up the phone and call her to say, "Guess what just happened." Since I started writing this book, however, speaking with her has been a lot easier. She and her husband are now back in the U.S. where he is training as a medic in Texas. Angie has always been around for me and I appreciate the years she has allowed me to lean on her shoulder for one catastrophe or another.

Despite how much love and respect you may feel for your friends, there is no love like the one you have for your family. I may not agree with everyone in my family, but I certainly do love each one. It is easy for me to love my family. I've known them all of my life. Some of my fondest memories of my family all center on the times we were all gathered together in one place. This was usually at Thanksgiving and Christmas. Thanksgiving was, and has always been, my favorite time of the year to spend with them.

There was a time when there were about twenty of us all under the age of fifteen. As the ruler, emperor, queen, and reigning head honcho of the family, my Granny made sure we all ate well and didn't destroy her carpet or her furniture. For fear of being yelled at, my aunts would gather all of us kids together in the kitchen for dinner. With so many kids at one time, the only real spot for us was the floor. Our "chair" and "tablecloth" were the early editions, late editions, and possibly last year's editions of any old newspaper my Granny had lying around. We would sip Koolaid from a plastic cup. Our utensils were definitely not Made in the USA, or even China. Our fingers served as the fork, knife, and spoon. These days, I've grown accustomed to using real forks and not relying on my fingers to enjoy collards. The best part of Thanksgiving, and any other big meal that we had, was Granny's homemade cakes and pies. To this day, I still can't figure out how she claimed her tasty treats were fat free, cholesterol free, sugar free, and free of any preservatives. Somehow, our hips and waistlines didn't get that memo.

My family took care of me, nurtured me, and watched me grow up. We had all kinds of family outings at the park, barbecues, brunches, and so forth. One thing people can truly say about my family is that no matter what's going on, you can depend on them for help whenever you need it. I never had to worry about anything as a child. I had a support system that was out of this world and family members who sometimes made me wonder if I was stuck in episodes of *Roseanne* or *Married With Children*. In a nutshell, we had fun and we still do.

Everyone had an opportunity to baby-sit me. Some babysitters were more memorable than others. My Aunt Viola would take me swimming, even though I didn't know how. One day we went to the swimming pool at Grant Park with her friend's daughter. I was brave and could handle the water, at least that's what I thought. When I got to the edge of the pool at the 4-foot marker, common sense said I should sit on the side and dangle my little feet over the granite edge to let the water cool my toes. Insanity, however, said I should jump right in and take my chances. Insanity, combined with gravity and the inability to swim, can be a real bitch, sometimes. After about three seconds of trying to figure out how to breathe under water and realizing it doesn't work that way, I had to be rescued by a nine year old. I'm not sure, but I probably got in trouble for that little escapade. If my mother didn't know about my little brush with death then, the cat's out of the bag now. She can't spank me now.

My cousin Betty is one of the more interesting people in the family. She would give me a bowl of vanilla ice cream and sit me in front of the television to watch cartoons all day. I was happy watching Tom and Jerry and the Pink Panther. One of the things I love about my cousin Betty is that no matter how old she gets, you will never know it. She will not hesitate to let you know she can do the electric slide, drop it like it's hot, and do the two-step with ease. I oftentimes have to warn my friends before they meet her. Whatever you do, I'd say, don't call her "ma'am" or you're likely to get your little feelings hurt.

My aunt Andrea, Betty's mother, is a little different. For some reason, she was the quiet, scary one during our childhood years. Could it have been her loud, piercing voice or her ability to just make little kids run away? I don't know, but I was scared. When my brother was still a toddler, he would crawl out of a hole that he somehow created in his play pen. Whenever Aunt Andrea came by, however, he would make a beeline for the pen. I never saw a little kid crawl so fast. If he had gone any faster, he would have left his Huggies behind.

Many of my family members loved me so much, they took it upon themselves to see to it that if I did something wrong, my backside would always remember not to do it again. I recall one incident when I was about eight years old. My mother and I visited my Aunt Emma in Madison, a small rural town about an hour and a half south of Atlanta. My cousin, Gary, and I became bored playing cops in the old barn behind their house. We decided it would be a great idea to play with matches inside his dad's old brown Chevrolet. I don't remember why that was such a good idea, but at eight years old, everything seemed fun. Our plan for excitement was foiled when we got caught. I never knew the painful sting of rawhide until that day and I chose not to become familiar with it again. Imagine being spanked with a 39-inch leather belt controlled by a 6'1", 250 pound man with the strength of a WWE wrestler.

That beat-down didn't seem to bother my cousin at all, but for me, it was an eye opening experience. It was like one of those after school specials in which the lesson to be learned was "don't play with matches in an old hoopty."

Unfortunately, my cousin Gary was killed a few years later by a drunk driver who ran the stop sign at a busy intersection in Decatur. For some reason, I couldn't bring myself to go to the funeral or I was simply not allowed to go. My aunt was devastated. That was in 1991. In 2005, my aunt Emma lost another son due to illness. No matter who you are or how many PhDs you may have in psychology, there is no way you can understand the pain of having to bury not one, but two of your children. The anger, frustration, and emotional fatigue are enough to drive a person to the edge of despair. Despite what she has gone through, she has been able to go through each day the best she can. For that, I greatly respect her and I admire her courage.

The greatest love I felt from my family, however, came from my mother and my grandmother. They have been the most inspirational women in my life for so many reasons. My mother worked all her life to be sure that my brother and I had everything we needed and some of the things we wanted. She spent nearly twenty-five years at Southern Bell, now called AT&T, and she even worked a few years at the City of Atlanta Police Department. We weren't the best kids in the world, but to my mother, we were her pride and joy. We made mistakes just like any other kids, but we were still her kids and the apple of her eye. Without my mother's guidance, I can honestly say I would be somewhere wasting away doing who knows what. Thanks to my mother, I was able to finish high school, attend college, and eventually go to graduate school. It wasn't her financial contributions that I am most thankful for. It was her constant support and encouragement for me to do well and be what I wanted to be. She is the greatest.

My grandmother, affectionately called "Granny" by the entire family and the neighborhood kids, passed away in November 1992 during the first semester of my freshman year in college. She had been sick for some time, but I didn't know exactly what was wrong because my family didn't really tell me. I guess they didn't want me to worry. She didn't have much, but whatever she could give, she would.

I remember the last time I saw her alive. It was a few days before my birthday in October and I came home for the weekend. I didn't know it at first, but while I was away at college in Macon, Georgia, my Granny was busy sewing a heavy quilt for me because I wrote her once to tell her how cold it was in my dorm room. The quilt was white with colorful shapes like flowers and butterflies in bright colors. The underside was dark purple. You could see the intricate stitching throughout the quilt. It must have taken days to complete. When I was younger, I remember sitting under the giant wooden square frame that she used as a guide to sew all of her quilts. I pretended I was an Indian chief sitting in my teepee watching *Mr. Rogers' Neighborhood*. Those were the good old days.

When she presented the quilt to me, she said, "I hope it keeps you warm." She then went to her secret blue dress in the closet, the one just behind her rifle and .22 pistol, pulled out her black wallet, and gave me two, crisp twenty-dollar bills. At that moment, all I could do was thank her, hug her, and tell her how much she and the quilt meant to me. For years, I never knew why Granny kept a rifle and a pistol in her closet. I didn't even know she knew how to operate one. I guess living in the country forces you to learn a lot about guns and how to shoot, especially during the early decades of the 20th century when the idea of gun control was not an issue.

There has been no woman in this world, other than my mother, I have loved more than my Granny. There has not been a single day since that dreary Thursday morning when we laid her to rest that I don't think about her. I can only hope that she's proud of her little "Toot" right now and that she knows that I'm okay. Oh yeah, I hope she knows that I haven't forgotten my promise to take care of my knucklehead brother. He, too, is doing well and is now starting his own family.

As I mentioned earlier, friends and family are very important and we mustn't discredit them for what they believe in. They are the ones who support and love us even when we are acting like real jerks. They stand by us no matter what. They support us and listen to us as we vent about our problems. In the past few years, I have leaned heavily on my friends and family, particularly Angie, my brother, and my mother, to help me through some of the tough relationships I have had. One of the things that really tickle me about my family is that they have never told me up front that they didn't like someone I was dating. Actually, my mother did say she couldn't stand one of the young ladies I introduced her to. She even went as far as to demand that I not bring her over again. That was a new side of her, but I liked it. I didn't particularly care for that chic either. I should have known from the moment I met her that she wasn't the bring-home-to-mama type of girl.

Overall, people in my family would hold their opinions to see how the relationship went and then make their comments. In the past three years and following the end of certain relationships, my family has used the following adjectives to describe the people I've introduced them to – vindictive, obnoxious, rude, arrogant, selfish, snooty, stubborn, bitchy, and my personal favorite, crazy as hell. So far, only one person has been able to get an "A" in their book. While our family members can still be good friends to us, there are, however, friends that we must be constantly aware of. I'm talking about the type of people we usually classify as mutual friends.

Sometimes we are introduced to people through our significant others. After a while, they become close enough to us that we are able to share certain things with them about our past, our feelings, and in some cases, our relationships. I had such friends in previous relationships. My sweetie introduced me to some of her friends. For a while, things between all of us were fine. We spent a lot of time together. We went to the movies, the park, concerts, and other events together. In the end, however, I realized that it is the mutual friends that give you the most problems. When things are going wrong in your relationship, mutual friends will almost always remain loyal to the people they knew first. They will stick by their side even if that friend is wrong. For example, they will cover up for their friend's whereabouts and act as an alibi whenever necessary. They will remain silent when their friend is being dishonest or is engaged in any activity that may reveal their friend as being unfaithful. The typical response a mutual friend will have is "it's not my business to say" or "I don't want to be in the middle of this." I guess I can't really fault them for that.

Best friends are the worse sometimes because they will, no matter what, remain silent in the face of deceit and betrayal. Now, I could care less what my any of my exes' best friends think of me or how their lives are going. As with any relationship, it is always best to let go of the people who either mean you harm or will do nothing to keep harm from coming to you. Whenever you see that your sweetie's best friends do not have your best interest in mind and is keeping quiet about certain things, let them go. One of the most important things you can learn from best friends is to never get too attached to them. The moment things begin to fall apart in your relationship, you will almost always be the last to know about it. Those so-called best friends will usually have first hand knowledge of everything and in some cases, have coached your sweetie on how not to be discovered if there is a major problem. I recall one of these so-called best friends played an active role in facilitating my sweetie's dishonesty. So, as I was talking to her and trying to understand what was going on with my sweetie, she already knew all the details and said nothing.

So ask yourself this – of the mutual friends you and your sweetie have and the people your sweetie call a best friend, how many of them do your really trust to be honest with you without regard to loyalty? My guess is that the number may be quite low. It's been my experience that sometimes these friends are able to keep certain things a secret because they, too, are involved in or have been involved in dishonest acts. This makes it easier for them to tell your sweetie what to do and what not to do. They are able to come up with the best lies in the world to cover up for just about any breach of fidelity or honesty in a relationship. For some reason, they may think it's fun to share the double-cheat approach to a relationship. I guess the old saying is true - birds of a feather flock together. The bottom line is that you should never get attached to your sweetie's best friend and don't give in to them when they say, "I had no clue" so-and-so was doing this or that. They know. Trust me.

Marriage, the Other Goliath

The United States is not ready to recognize same sex marriage. The people that are elected to represent this country feel that same sex marriage is a threat to family values and sends the wrong message to children. What about the messages clergymen send their congregation and society as a whole when it's revealed that they molested young children? What about the messages that husbands send when they verbally and physically abuse their wives or even molest their own children? What about the messages men send when they attempt to have sex with a minor and are caught on shows like *Dateline NBC* and others? These issues are more of a threat to family values and impact children more than same sex marriage does. So what are these elected officials really scared of?

Homosexuals should be allowed to get married and experience the same benefits as any other married couple, including health coverage, social security benefits, tax benefits, and so on. Politicians feel same sex marriage is immoral and should only be defined as a union between one man and one woman. Some people say that if homosexuals want to enjoy all the benefits of a heterosexual marriage, then they should marry someone of the opposite sex. If I'm not mistaken, that defeats the purpose of being gay. What may eventually come out of this way of thinking is an influx of gay men and gay women rushing to marry each other for the purpose of equality and recognition only. Love, in this case, is not a prerequisite neither is living together as if they were married. Compare this to many people from third world who marry Americans just to have citizenship rights in the U.S.

Again, where is the threat to traditional marriages? I don't see it. If John and Jack decide they want to get married, how would their union hurt, hinder, or become a nuisance to Jim and Mary's marriage? In the 60s and 70s, the United States denied interracial couples the right to marry. Perhaps it will take a few more years for the U.S. to adopt same sex marriage policies like Canada and some European countries. As long as there are legitimate churches and other organizations across the nation that cater to our needs, there will still be civil unions that will allow same sex couples to be joined in a lifetime partnership with one another. There will also be attorneys willing to devise power of attorneys, trusts, wills, partnership agreements, and other important documents that will allow same sex couples to protect their assets and in some ways, validate their relationship in the public eye.

When you're married, you are automatically obligated to give 100% of yourself to the other person. You are obligated to make things work at any cost. It's like a contract where each person is essentially a partner and has certain duties to fulfill as part of that contract. If you break the contract, you risk losing the trust, commitment, and support of your mate.

While I didn't have a traditional marriage, I had a wife. In fact, I've been married twice. Let's just say my ex-wives names were Rose and Delilah. In each relationship, we talked on the phone for a while before we even met. I was completely blown away by Rose. She was the Goliath in my life for a number of years as I was deeply in love with her. There was a connection between us from the moment we said "hello." I felt she was the only one in the world that could make me happy. She believed in me; trusted me, and without a doubt, cared for me. She supported me and along every step of the way, she was by my side. Seeing her smile was like being on a beautiful beach at sunset watching the waves crash into one another. Like Helen of Troy, she had a smile that could launch a trillion ships. Her personality was charming, friendly, and above all, genuine. She had a way of making the people around her feel good. She was very spiritual, intelligent, and talented. Even today, I would do anything for her although she and I are not together. But, who knows what could have been. I hope that she is doing well wherever she may be.

Our relationship was a special one. We talked about everything under the sun – work, school, family, and so on. Before we knew it, the night had turned into day and we were still talking. Our conversation was unique. It flowed from subject to subject without a pause. We had to meet. When I first saw her, I thought she was beautiful and had a gorgeous smile. I was scared to give her a hug and even more scared to actually kiss her. I thought she might turn away and want to run, but I'm glad she didn't.

Delilah was almost a complete opposite. Initially, she was sweet and quenched my thirst for love and romance. I could talk to her about anything. She, too, had a beautiful smile and a great personality. Over time, things changed. Our relationship was nothing like it was before. Problems soon plagued the relationship to the point where I did whatever I could just to keep the peace. I let my love for her overshadow my own happiness.

My mother and Granny raised me to always speak politely about people. If you can't say anything polite or be respectful, change the conversation or walk away. At this point, however, there are no nice words I can say about Delilah. With that in mind, I will take their advice and put this part of the discussion on a brief hiatus until a later time. I hope I do not offend you, gracious readers, in any way by doing so.

I would like to reiterate my belief that homosexuals should be given the same marriage rights as everyone in this country. At the same time, I am concerned that some women in the lesbian community are oblivious to what it means to be married to another woman. It means a lot more than just being able to call someone your wife. It's about more than just exchanging gold or platinum rings that are supposed to symbolize your unending love for one another. Being married is about a whole lot more than just being able to tell your friends that your "player card" has now been retired and that you're officially off the market. Some people actually believe that all you have to do to be married is just say a few sweet words in your living room and let that be it. For some, an informal proclamation of love and commitment such as this is okay. But for others, it is necessary to go through the steps that are required to be married in order to make your relationship seem more valid. Marriage in the homosexual community takes more effort and more patience in order to make it work.

In our community, marriage is extremely overrated and is oftentimes misinterpreted. The lifelong union of same-gendered individuals is not called a marriage, bur rather a civil union. Civil unions are created via a commitment ceremony which is facilitated by an ordained minister of the couple's choosing. The minister may have his or her beliefs based on the foundations of various denominations including Baptist, Episcopalian, Methodist, and so on. It's important to remember that not every religious faction will condone such unions so finding a minister can be difficult. In planning a commitment ceremony, the couple may opt to hire someone who specializes in planning ceremonies of this nature or they are able to choose for themselves every facet of the event – time, place, decorations, music, the people involved, etc. For simplicity sake, I have chosen to use the term marriage and civil union interchangeably along with the terms wedding and commitment ceremony throughout this book.

The most important thing I would like to target here is counseling. For many people, heterosexuals and homosexuals, a series of counseling sessions is not only recommended, but in some cases are required. As I think back to my counseling sessions, there are so many things that came to the surface. You learn so much about yourself and the person you are about to pledge the rest of your life to. Some of the issues that came up in my sessions had to do with sex, infidelity, role-playing, insecurities, pet peeves, goals, and a lot of other things.

One of the most important things you learn in counseling is whether the two of you are actually emotionally prepared for such a venture as marriage. You also learn if the person you are about to marry is the right person for you. For some people, counseling is needed at the beginning, middle, and if necessary, toward the end of a relationship. If counseling is needed towards the end of the relationship, it may not necessarily be too late to rebuild the relationship. In other cases, however, counseling may seem like a waste of time because one party refuses to take part in the process, one party is simply going through the motions just to say she tried, or the relationship is not worth saving anymore.

When you are just dating someone, it is not hard to say to your mate that you want to terminate the relationship and begin seeing other people. There is no obligation for you to stay. There is nothing to hold you back. There is nothing keeping you tied to a woman who you no longer care about and no longer want to be involved in an intimate relationship with. You have the right to walk away. When you're married, however, you are bound by certain conventions that make it almost impossible for you to just turn and leave.

For me, my marriage to Delilah was more or less like being an inmate in a state prison. For some reason, I was sentenced to only be around her and not socialize with friends and family as much as I wanted. Rather than express how I felt about certain things, I remained silent. Isolation became my only option so I turned to writing. My thoughts and feelings were no longer my own; everything was based on someone else's response. If my actions did not match up with how she would do things, I was wrong. Great care and concern preceded any statement that had to do with my dislikes and desires. Most often, I just felt it was better to remain quiet and keep everything to myself in order to avoid an argument. At one point, things became very predictable and in some cases, amusing. I recall arguments started happening every month on the same date for three months straight. I just expected them and in some strange, twisted way, looked forward to the next big insignificant quarrel. I don't remember what the arguments were about. They just happened. I began to wonder if the arguments were somehow related to some premenstrual phenomenon. It's not a good thing when you look forward to an argument. I was actually disappointed when there was not an argument on the fourth month.

If you are interested in getting married, just know that Marriage, the other great Goliath, is one of those things that like Love can have power over you. Marriage can't function without Love and together, Love and Marriage act as twin forces against you. As I mentioned earlier, Love can make you do some crazy things. Marriage, however, can make you really test your faithfulness. Depending on the person, Marriage can make you remain faithful or test the waters to see what else is out there. Marriage is an institution that seeks to bind two people together forever. Some people are able to live with one another and share each other's passions, hopes, and desires for a lifetime. This takes a great deal of commitment. At other times, Marriage can make you wish for the single life again.

Marriage, then, can have the same effects on a person as Love. Because we put so much value on Marriage, it is oftentimes looked upon in a negative light to terminate that relationship. However, there is only so long you can stay in a relationship you don't want to be in. There is only so much you can take. Marriage will sometimes force you to believe that you have an obligation to stay married rather than leave. But I, like the illustrious poet John

47

Dryden wrote in his play, *Marriage a la Mode*, believe that when you're not happy, "why should a foolish marriage vow/which long ago was made/oblige us to each other now/when passion is decayed" (Hunter, p. 24). Marriage forces you to believe that without that relationship, you will never be whole again because you'll be without your so-called "soul mate." Be careful. Marriage can trick you into thinking that it, too, like Love, is the most wonderful thing in the world. I say that it's not, but to those who want it, good luck to you in your quest.

At this time in my life, I have no desire or plans to ever connect myself hip-to-hip again with that Goliath, Marriage. I don't want to put myself in the position of going through the process of proving myself to others again. I don't want to worry about what someone else is doing with her life and how those choices affect me as well. I don't want to have to deal with anyone's insecurities about my whereabouts and who I choose to associate with. I don't want to feel obligated to one person for the rest of my life. Life is too short and to be in a place where you don't want to be in is not good at all. I don't want to be Marriage's inmate again. I don't want to be tied down to another Delilah. I'm not curious enough to find out if the third time really will be the last time. Besides, Marriage is not a universal vaccine against infidelity and will not fill some sort of void that you feel is plaguing your life.

On the Fence

A fence is another way of establishing distance between two people. So, if your sweetie says, "I don't know what I want, I'm on the fence," accept the fact that your sweetheart is playing you. No matter how long you have been in a relationship with your sweetheart, do not accept that she's on the fence about anything. When she says she's on the fence, it implies a dilemma in which the answer is already known, but is yet to be formally communicated to you. Question her and when you get an answer, question her again. Our current legal system recognizes this type of questioning as the Socratic Method. Every question and answer leads to another question and answer until there is only one finite response.

I was once given the "I'm on the fence" speech. At first, I was shocked and had many questions. How could you not know what you want? "I'm just confused," she says and follows up with "I can't think right now." I wondered how hard is it to decide to be honest with someone about your intentions. For some people, however, the choice is always crystal clear – maintain secrecy. Unless the topic is about who will make dinner tonight or which movie to see at the local theater, the answer should never involve straddling an imaginary fence pondering not if, but when the game of deception should be over.

A fence straddler is a dangerous person when it comes to relationships. She will seldom make a decision that will impact the security of her relationship so that she can explore her selfish desires with someone else. In other words, a fence straddler may say why give up Mama's famous peach cobbler that you have been addicted to for years when you can have it and Breyer's Ice Cream to make the whole dessert better. To say that she's on the fence is the politically correct way of your sweetie saying she's cheating on you, but that she wants you to believe that she isn't. At least for a while longer.

It's a generally accepted rule that if a person continuously accuses you of something that you know you haven't done, the chances are she has already committed the same act that she accuses you of. One of my exes lived by that

49

rule and swore it was possibly the best piece of truth in the world. I found out the hard way that she had proven her theory was correct.

In one of my relationships, my significant other always accused me of cheating. Coworkers and other people that I spoke with from time to time were not just friends in her eyes; they were objects of my affection and a threat to our relationship. She reached this erroneous conclusion based on the fact that I did not want to engage in certain activities, go certain places, or speak with certain people. The problem here was that there were other things going on in our relationship and she was incapable of grasping how those things affected certain areas of our relationship. I know now that some people only want to believe what they see and not give any consideration to other important factors.

When it comes to relationships, unless your friends have done anything to violate the boundaries of your relationship with your sweetheart, keep them close. If they are genuine friends that you can trust and are willing to share some of your darkest secrets with them, cherish them. I once had a small group of friends I hung out with prior to getting involved in one particular relationship. My friends and I went out to various clubs, sporting events, and other popular hangouts. My sweetheart at the time thought that it was not a good idea to spend so much time with my friends. I thought this strange because every minute of the day, it seemed, I was with her. She, by her own admission, was jealous of the time I spent with others and did not want to accept the fact that there were times when I wanted to be around other people. The nerve of me to have such needs! How dare I want some "me" time to escape from her jealousy.

If your sweetheart asks you to choose between her and the small number of good friends that you have, know that her request goes beyond ridiculous. People need to have the strength and support of friends. People need to discuss things with their friends and get some sort of clarity, especially if it has to do with their sweetheart. You can't always talk to your sweetheart about what's bothering you. You need to be able to call your friend and say, "John, let me tell you how Mary just pissed me off!" Believe it or not, this helps to create healthy relationships, not destroy them. Keeping a person's real friends away from them, especially if they were friends before the sweetheart came along, is not a good idea. It's those friends who are eagerly waiting for you to leave the house to come over for some "friendly" conversation or late night hours to text your sweetheart to say, "good night" that you have to worry about. It's those friends you see making your sweetheart a candlelight dinner for no reason that you have to worry about. You should definitely be cautious when your sweetheart insists that you go to work. It could be just another way of her having the house all to herself for some reason. In essence, this all seems like the epitome of a double standard. Things should never be acceptable for one person to do and unacceptable for the other person to do.

I was in a situation like this before and it was not anything I would want even my worse enemy to endure. Certain friends of mine, and even coworkers, were looked upon as being people I was greatly attracted to or vice versa. However, her friends were considered just friends. Any ordinary lesbian with at least a high school education who witnessed first hand her sweetheart on the phone at 3 AM, text messages at different times of the night, and sudden trips at 1 AM with no real explanation would come to the conclusion that the sweetheart is a liar. Going back to one of the biggest truths of the world according to my ex, on everything that is genuine and true and real in my life, I never cheated on her. No matter how many problems she and I had, I never stepped outside the bounds of our relationship. I guess at times, things may have appeared otherwise, but when a person already has trust issues, I guess it's difficult to make them believe anything you say.

So, don't accept your mate as being "on the fence." The fence is just an excuse. Your sweetie's so-called fence represents an easy way out. For her, the fence is a way to see how green the neighbor's grass is while keeping her own lawn in tact. When we think of fences, we see an intertwined wall of steel, wood panels, or other material that separate one piece of property from another. In relationships, the purpose of a fence is no different. On one side of the fence is your committed wife, girlfriend, or fiancé. There may be some issues or problems in the relationship that may cause one person to take a look at what's going on in the neighbor's yard. If you've ever seen Tim Allen's *Tool Time*, then you will remember the family has a neighbor, Wilson, on the other side of a wooden fence. Wilson never shows anything but his nose, eyes, and hat if he's wearing one. Allen and Wilson always talk to each other, but no one ever really makes a leap over the fence.

What makes a person take that leap? Frustration, curiosity, anger, bitterness, and revenge can all play a role in that decision. Sometimes it's the thrill of having someone on the side. More often than not, it's to fulfill a need for sexual satisfaction. The consequences for taking that leap can be huge and may even greatly damage a relationship. To straddle that fence means you are willing to accept the consequences despite what it could do to your relationship. People who take these leaps of insanity are not always aware of the people they hurt. They are in it for themselves. They want to satisfy their own needs regardless of yours. Sometimes they just want to see how far they can go before they cause you to be at your absolute breaking point.

Know the warning signs of a fence straddler. First, she will be evasive in answering your questions or she may answer your questions with a question. Second, she may spend a lot of unnecessary time with the person on the other side of that fence and claim that "she's just a friend." Third, you may notice that your relationship has taken a turn for the worse and in the middle of it all is the person on the other side of the fence. Fourth, if you and your sweetheart have joint accounts, watch out for sudden changes in your partner's spending habits when it comes to the person on the other side of the fence. Fifth, she will deny the fact that she has an interest in anyone else, but her actions will say otherwise. Last, pay close attention to how her behavior changes. Is she going out more and staying out late? Does she give you off the wall excuses for where she was or who she was with?

51

There are other signs as well. When you recognize them, it means it's time to move on. Help her over the fence with a solid, relentless push. When she's gone, don't look back. Just listen for the thud she will make when she eventually realizes that her decision to jump the fence was a tragic mistake.. In time, she will notice that the neighbor's house isn't always the best house. If I had done that, I would have saved myself a lot of heartache. I saw things happening before me and brought them to her attention. There is not much you can say when a fence straddler has already made up her mind. She wants the thrill and excitement of having a relationship outside the boundaries of a committed relationship and the security of the person to whom she has pledged herself, body and soul. It can't be that way. Run, my friend, run! She is not worth your time.

In a sense, I created an imaginary fence for myself at various times. I envisioned myself dating again. I pictured myself being happy once again with someone I could trust. I envisioned my life without my sweetie. Imagination can be a wonderful thing as it takes you to a world outside yourself to one that is most beautiful to you. I longed for that place in real life. Unfortunately, imagination is not reality. At the end of each day, my fence was torn down and I was unwillingly taken back to the place I didn't want to be in and to be with people I wanted to forget. Instead, all I could do was peer through the holes in the fence and wonder "what if?"

PART 2:

LIBERATION

Since there's not help, come let us kiss and part,
Nay, I am done, you get no more of me;
And I am glad, yea, glad with all my heart,
That thus so cleanly I myself can free;
Shake hands for ever, cancel all our vows,
And when we meet at any given time again,
Be it not seen in either of our brows
That we, one jot of former love retain
~ Michael Drayton
"Farewell to Love"

On Freedom and Liberation

America is obsessed with freedom and will do whatever it takes to protect it. The notion of protecting and ensuring freedom in America has been prevalent ever since the original thirteen colonies made their argument for independence from British rule over two hundred years ago. In *The Declaration of Independence*, Thomas Jefferson wrote:

> When in the course of human events, it becomes necessary for one people to dissolve the political bonds which have connected them with another, and to assume among the powers of the earth, the separate and equal station to which the laws of nature and of nature's God entitle them...

Jefferson's argument for independence from British rule suggests that in order for a nation to thrive, it must be able to govern itself and not be bound by the rules and limitations of other nations. It must maintain sovereignty over its own affairs and govern its people in a manner that promotes prosperity and peace. Jefferson's basic tenet was freedom is essential to achieve this goal.

What is freedom and why is it so important to us today? According to Webster's New World Dictionary, freedom is an ease of movement or feeling of independence. For example, the First Amendment guarantees us the right to free, or independent, expression of religion and speech so long as the rights of others are not infringed upon. We have the freedom to move and live anywhere we want so long as we meet certain eligibility criteria. We are free to love whomever we want to love. So, freedom is more or less a right to do something, but it sometimes involves certain limitations that are based on personal preferences, rules, and regulations. Freedom, although limited in some cases, is important to us today because it allows us the opportunity to express our ideas, achieve whatever goals we have set for ourselves, and set ourselves apart from others.

Liberate, on the other hand, means to set free or release someone or something. For example, after the Civil War, Negroes were released from the bonds of slavery through the Thirteenth Amendment, but they were not totally free. They could not truly vote without race-based limitations until years later and in some cases, were still tied to their slave masters through sharecropping. Similarly, a person may be released from jail after serving his sentence for a felonious offense, but he may not have the same freedom he once held. In some cases, he loses his freedom to vote in state and federal elections, obtain federal loans, attend school, live in certain areas of the state, or obtain a sustainable means of employment.

While freedom is an important aspect of American politics and culture, it is not the same as being liberated. A person is actually liberated when she is able to permanently release certain people and things from her mind and her spirit that are hindrances to her success. A liberated mind gives a person the freedom to go anywhere and do anything. She is capable of overcoming her past, learning from prior mistakes, accepting certain things as losses, and moving forward in the direction in which she is called.

A person who is liberated from bad relationships has learned how to overcome some of the challenges associated with them. She has somehow realized her true value and knows that she deserves happiness. A liberated person is able to walk away from certain people in her life with confidence. A liberated person is strong, determined, and capable of achieving anything in life. A liberated person is able to forgive those who have hurt her in the past, lied to her, or who have in some way mistreated her. A liberated person is honest and firm in her convictions. She is trustworthy. She is a leader and an agent of change. A liberated person is without doubt, one of the most dangerous people in the world because she refuses to be left behind and she refuses to accept mediocrity in her work and her personal affairs.

Liberation is important in certain relationships. Consider, for example, the woman who is abused by her mate and has to hide her bruises on a daily basis. Consider someone who has to constantly hide her sadness in order to keep peace in her home. Consider the woman who is in a relationship she no longer feels is healthy for her to be a part of. In my case, I was in relationships that were not good at all for various reasons. In each of these examples and in mine, someone is trapped in a place that is dark, lonely, and scary. It is a place overwhelmed with uncertainty. Unfortunately, there are so many cases in which people will stay in these relationships. There are people who sit back and watch terrible things happen without taking a stand against them.

When a person finally realizes its time to move forward, it creates what some people might call an emotional breakthrough. When a person is liberated and frees herself from the past, her mindset begins to completely change. You will see people taking their lives into their own hands rather than subjecting themselves to someone else's whims and thought processes. A liberated person is happier and is rarely able to contain her excitement. She is strength personified. There is nothing that can be done to deter her from her goal. I am reminded of a song by Keith Urban called *"You'll Think of Me."* In this song, Urban proclaims, "While you're sleeping with your pride/Wishing I could hold you tight/I'll be over you/And on with my life." This is what a liberated person will be bold enough to say to people in her past. She will look at them and not be moved to anger or frustration. She will not be moved to think about how so-and-so hurt her or the things that so-and-so said in the past.

This is my goal for people who have experienced any of the things I speak about in this book.. It is my goal for people to not be afraid of the world outside their relationships. It is my goal for people to understand that a relationship should not be a prison, but rather something that enables people to share themselves physically and emotionally with someone who share the dream of happiness and liberation.

The Milk Is Sour

A few months ago, I decided to go to The Vision Church (TVC) in Atlanta to hear my pastor give one of his exciting sermons. It had been a few weeks since I last visited so I was anxious to get there. I was having a difficult week and needed to have some spiritual nourishment and fellowship from my church family. I knew I could count on a good word and fellowship from TVC because I had been receiving it every time I visited. After a few announcements and a little anecdote about him accidentally drinking milk that had spoiled in his refrigerator, the pastor said something that really amazed and puzzled me. It was also something I will never forget. Paraphrasing the pastor, any relationship that goes beyond its expiration date has the potential to spoil your life.

What in the world did he mean? I don't confess to being the Einstein of my village as there are some things I just don't understand despite the academic accolades that hang on my wall. There was something in his speech, however, that just didn't make it to my brain for quick translation. It took a few minutes for me to understand the concept, but after a few more congregational "Amens" and "Uh-huhs," I got it.

People are placed in our lives for only a set period of time and for a particular purpose. Sometimes they are in our lives for a lifetime and they may actually be our soul mates. Sometimes, they are in our lives for just a moment in time, but we are attracted to one another in such a way, that we become one in the same. Some people are in our lives to help us, hinder us, challenge us, and so on. Whether the purpose has a negative or positive connotation, there is always a set time period for them to be with us. It could be five minutes, five months, five years, or forever. We can not determine the time limit on our own. To go beyond that time period sets us up for what could be a dangerous fall and harsh lessons in life we may not necessarily be able to fully appreciate, but we are forced to learn. This actually happened to me.

I was in a relationship with someone I thought I would be with in my old age. We seemed right for one another and the time we spent together was, for the most part, enjoyable. At some point, the challenges began. There were moments in our relationship where we each questioned if we should continue or not. For me, I knew I wasn't happy and that I wanted out for a long time. I was tired of the strain on our ability to communicate with one another. I was tired of the arguing. I was tired of the jealousy. I was, in fact, tired of her. But I stayed. I was forcing something to work that was not destined to be a lifetime commitment.

We've all had relationships that didn't work. We put forth our best efforts and tried desperately to salvage what was left. Unfortunately, there comes a time when we have to say goodbye, or free ourselves from that relationship. The expiration date has arrived and it's time to get rid of the old or replace it. What makes this a difficult task is when we've been in that relationship for a number of years. Sometimes life's events prove themselves a gun aiming straight at our temple, forcing us to make quick decisions or subject ourselves to further disappointments and regrets.

Letting go of a relationship is done for many reasons and in many different ways. A person can let go by ending the relationship without cause. Perhaps one person is just not willing to be tied down to one person anymore. A relationship can be terminated due to infidelity, dishonesty, and mistrust. Financial worries, problems with intimacy, so-called friends, and a host of other reasons all play a part in the ultimate decision to end a relationship. Sometimes we just simply become bored with the person we're with and are anxiously waiting for a way out of the nightmare.

Terminating a relationship is not always the worse thing that could possibly happen. Sometimes it's best for both parties to have, if possible, an amicable separation. I was more than thankful one of my relationships ended. Unfortunately, I didn't realize how beneficial it was to me to not have this person in my life. She and I had been slowly drifting apart for a while. There were some serious issues that plagued our relationship. Despite my quiet state of unhappiness, I remained faithful to her. The expiration date for our relationship had long since passed, but I was still sipping on bad milk.

What causes us to stay in a relationship we don't want to be in? For me, a part of it had to do with fear. I had some insecurities and I didn't like the idea of facing the unknown alone. Would I be okay? Could I do this alone? So many questions inundated my mind and yet the answers came slowly and far between. I felt trapped because I didn't know what to do. I quickly learned how to deal with my unhappiness by not confronting the source of my unhappiness. What I learned from this experience was that it was not the person I was with that I was trying to cling to. It was the security of that relationship that meant more to me. When it comes to moving on to new relationships, Maxine Schnall writes, "the loss of structure in the gap between the end of one phase…and the beginning of the next provokes intense anxiety, too. But you have to remember that structure is all you've lost—you haven't lost your life" (Schnall, p. 112).

In many of my relationships, I liked the fact that someone else knew exactly what I liked on my burger. I liked the fact that I had someone to come home to each day. I liked the fact that someone, according to her own admissions, loved and cared for me. As problems became more and more prevalent in our relationship, those things were not enough anymore. I had to step away or continue to put my life on hold.

When you are ready to move on, you will know. It's important to take the first step, but do it in a manner that is proper so that no one is hurt any more than she has to be. In one of my relationships, letting go was hard to do because I didn't follow my own rules of disengagement, which I will discuss later. But, we all know that hindsight is 20/20. Even when I saw she was trying to have her cake and eat it, too, I still didn't let go. Perhaps it was because I had spent too much time in the relationship. For the most part, I think it was because I was scared, but I'm not sure what I was scared about.

Going back to Pastor's comments, I didn't toss the old milk. Instead of tossing the milk that had obviously gone past its expiration date, I tried to extract some goodness therein. I smelled the unpleasant odor. I knew the expiration date had passed, but I continued to hold on to that milk for a few more weeks. To me, it didn't taste spoiled; my mouth didn't pucker up as if I had tasted a tangy lemon. It didn't look spoiled. It didn't say "don't drink me" past a certain time. All it said was "drink me, and I will satisfy your thirst." In my mind, it was still Mayfield in the yellow one-gallon plastic container with the little brown cow on the front label.

I should have let her go. I should have discarded her the minute I saw changes beginning to happen. I should have heightened my senses in such a way that I could recognize that while this looks good and tastes good and feels good, this woman is not right. We reached our expiration date, but I didn't move on to new milk soon enough. When you continue to stay in a relationship that has gone past its expiration date, you can become ill in your body as if you did drink a container of bad milk. If you stay in that relationship long enough and are unhappy and miserable, feelings of resentment, anger, disappointment, and isolation can be manifested in a number of ways. You may experience frequent headaches, chest pains, loss of sexual desire, and other ailments. You may even find it difficult to talk to one another or be in the same room with one another. You may not want to talk to her on the phone as every phone call is an interruption in your daily moment of peace and tranquility. For me, it was more enjoyable to enjoy a quiet lunch alone than to call my sweetie just to say hello. Feelings like these are not healthy and should be immediately addressed.

You must leave a bad relationship before it buries you. You must deal with your fears and reservations in such a way that you are able to recognize the fact that leaving is the best alternative and will minimize the emotional stress and bodily ailments you may be experiencing. When you continue to stay in a relationship you no longer want to be in, everything can become a much greater strain including conversation and intimacy. All that is required for you to do is just take the first step. Ask yourself one question. Is it better for you to feel hurt and pain in your body by staying with someone you don't want to be with or is it better to take your chances and experience fresh milk somewhere else? I don't know about you, but I would rather enjoy the freshness of a new, more positive relationship rather than be stuck somewhere I don't belong. Think about what's more important to you and go for it. Once you become too comfortable in the relationship, leaving it makes things more difficult.

Women Do It Better

It amazes me how many women there are out there who are actually engaged in down-low relationships. Usually when you hear someone being on the down-low, the first thing that comes to mind is heterosexual men who have intimate relationships with other men without their girlfriends, wives, or families knowing about it. But now, there is a new, more complicated breed of down-lowers – women in the homosexual community. They definitely have the down-low system on lock and are able to perpetrate several relationships at one time. They're able to juggle work, a family, and several relationships in a single bound. Perhaps it has something to do with the fact that women are just naturally more cunning than men and are able to multitask a lot better than our male counterparts. Who knows?

In the past few years, I have heard some women refer to themselves as a "playa," "pimp," "hustler," and my favorite, "gangsta of love." Usually these terms are used by younger lesbians who do not yet realize or are completely oblivious to the fact that these self-proclaimed labels are neither complimentary nor endearing terms. Negative terms like these go beyond a person's age and extend to an entire group of people within the lesbian community. These are the people who take it upon themselves to step outside the confines of a monogamous relationship to entertain and satisfy their own selfish, egotistical curiosities. It is this group of people I feel I have an obligation to address at this moment for so many reasons.

Women who cheat begin and end each day being intimately involved with someone who is not their wife or girlfriend. They call each other in the wee hours of the morning or late at night hoping not to be discovered. They make it a point to hide in the bathroom, careful to turn on the shower so that their sleeping partner can't hear a word. They whisper when they talk to the outsider, but yell like they are in the middle of a rock concert when they're talking to everyone else in the world. When you're in the next room, they cover their head with a blanket and pillow just to engage in conversation with the outsider. With the convenience of unlimited text messaging, email, and instant messenger capabilities, these women will play out their fantasies, schedule a

61

secret rendezvous, and exchange various cutsies all with the touch of a few buttons. I am so glad that technology has made it possible to bring these soaring, yet scandalous and unconscionable, love birds together! I'm overrun with such emotion. Please pass me a Kleenex.

Women cheat on their partners every day. Even as you read this book, there is a woman out there somewhere, perhaps in your town or in the apartment next door to you, who may have just experienced an overwhelmingly intense orgasm caused by someone who is not her wife or girlfriend even though she is in a relationship with someone else. There could also be a woman sitting at a local Starbucks café drinking coffee waiting for her blind date, a young sexy lady she spoke with on a chat line who claims she will be wearing a pink bow on the left side of her hair. She has to be careful, though. She doesn't want anyone to drive by and see her in the middle of the afternoon when she should be at work. Maybe there is a secret romance brewing right in your office between two people who claim they are just friends.

Unless we are absent from our mind in some fashion or another, we all recognize and accept the fact that people cheat on their wives or girlfriends all the time. The act is fairly common despite our beliefs that monogamy is one of the most important keys to a long, successful relationship and an excellent defense against sexually transmitted diseases. Nonetheless, our culture is slowly moving from the "until death do us part" approach to marriage and lifelong commitment to a mode of operation that is more appropriately defined by the phrase, "until caught in the act" (Barondess, p. 57). This definitely includes women in the homosexual and heterosexual community.

I still can't understand why people cheat. If you're not happy in a relationship, leave. If you want to see other people, admit your desires, sever any ties you have with your current wife or girlfriend, and go on about your business. Unfortunately, most women don't believe in doing things in an orderly fashion. They prefer to create chaos because that's the mindset they're in at the time. They like the adventure and excitement that comes with "playing the field." I know several women who are like this. They are so far removed from reality that to bring them back to the real world and show them the folly of their actions would be a challenge in itself.

Perhaps I'm asking too much. What's wrong with wanting to be done with one relationship before starting another? Nothing. However, you will find that many women enjoy the satisfaction they get out of cheating on their mates. They enjoy keeping their mates in the dark. They enjoy inflicting some level of pain or hurt on the person they're with. Sometimes it's just a matter of making someone jealous. Some women are just bitter and I will touch on this later. Some women feel they have found love in someone else. I say that, too, is bull.

When we think of someone cheating, it sometimes has to do with sexual gratification and lack of self esteem more than anything else. In her book, *Gay Relationships,* Tina Tessina suggests "while excitement about and strong sexual urges toward a lover can be simply a positive indication of physical and emotional attraction, they can also be signs of unresolved inner conflicts for which we are seeking resolution. We all fantasize about love, but for some of us the myth obscures the reality" (Tessina, p. 67). In other words, women who cheat are oftentimes disillusioned and get lust and revenge confused with love and moral responsibility.

Right now, I want to speak directly to the cheater and the so-called other woman or outsider. I hope that as you read these lines, you consider what I have to say. I don't expect anyone to confess to their mates that they cheated. I do expect you to at least be honest with yourself since you can't be honest with your mate.

I have to ask. Are you a coward? If you were not a coward, it wouldn't have been hard for you to say to your mate you want to see other people. Are you cheating because you're compensating for not being able to sexually satisfy your mate? Some people get off on being able to tell their friends they have two or three girlfriends. It makes them seem bigger than they really are. Is that you? Why are you afraid to be with just one person? Have you been so hurt in the past that you don't want to be faithful to anyone? Are you one of those women who enjoy having the safety and security of a stable relationship while enjoying the thrill of a younger woman? Perhaps you're just in a place right now where you want to take advantage of people before they take advantage of you. It could just be that you're selfish and lack any sense of moral responsibility. Isn't it hard trying to maintain some type of balance between your home life and that part of you that you share with an outsider? Do you ever get scared of getting caught? What would happen if you did get caught and your sweetie turned into some Lynn Whitfield type of character from *It's a Thin Line Between and Hate?* The most important question is do you see yourself with the outsider in the next year or even five years? How much different do you think your life will be with this person as opposed to without her?

If you're the other woman, how would you feel if someone destroyed your relationship? How would you feel if someone was contacting your sweetie in the middle of the night or using your hard earned money to fund dinner dates and movie nights with someone else? How would you feel knowing the person you're creeping with was still being intimate with the person she cheated on to be with you? How would you feel if all of a sudden, you found out there is another woman? Would you be upset? Would you just brush it off as if you didn't care? My guess is that you don't care. Regardless of whether or not you have been abused, mistreated, or even cheated on in the past, what gives you the right to continue in that same mode of thinking that it's okay to disrupt lives? Has someone given you the authority to seek vengeance on your ex by inflicting the same type of dishonesty in someone else's relationship? What joy do you get out of possibly destroying a relationship? How does it benefit you to see one person being betrayed as a result of your words and actions? Are you, too, scared of being hurt and would rather inflict pain before it is inflicted upon you? Perhaps you are not mature enough, despite your age, to realize that what goes around comes around.

63

In the past few years, I have seen and heard so much along the line of cheaters. I've heard stories of people who have gone on dinner dates in the evening with one woman and attended a late night party with another on the same day. I've heard stories of how the other woman was upset that her sweetie was having sex with someone else in their home. One of my personal favorites is the story I heard about how the cheating girlfriend wanted her mate to pay certain bills while she continued to entertain the other woman. She had some nerve. Now that was a knee-slapper. I can't forget to mention the story about the young lady who was in a car accident and was badly injured. Her mate was notified, but where was she? Only she and God knew for sure. She never showed up as her girlfriend was being prepped for surgery. My guess is that she wasn't just stuck in traffic.

To you, it may be the "in" thing to cheat. It may mean the difference between you being hurt and you hurting someone else. Cheating, however, is not all it's cracked up to be. You must understand that any relationship that starts in chaos, dishonesty, and deception will ultimately be plagued by those same things and will eventually end the same way. If you are one of those cheaters who want to have sex with the other woman and the woman you cheated on, something is definitely wrong with you. For you, it's all a game. You want to see who will come out victorious. You enjoy being at the center of everyone's affection. You, my friend, are nothing shy of manipulative and cunning. You don't care about yourself, your body, or the position you put others in. You are essentially leading a double life, which requires much skill and quick thinking. According to Dr. Shirley Glass, it requires "managing the logistics, including erasing e-mails, hiding cell phones, camouflaging expenses; meeting sites have to be convenient but not places you will likely encounter people you know. The emotional effort of sustaining two relationships, neither of which can be totally authentic, is also difficult. Lying not only erodes personal integrity, it distances you from the person you are lying to….there are two people to deceive" (Glass, p. 59)

When you cheat on someone, you do more than just cause people not to trust you. You create an environment in which people may begin to completely resent you or, for lack of a better term, hate you. People tend to wonder why your personality and everything you do are completely different. Granted, sometimes change is good, but there is such a thing as changing for the worse. This is what happens when you cheat. You cause your friends to be put in the difficult position of covering for you when you want to sow your wild oats. You put them in the middle of your chaotic escapades. You cause family members to worry about you and wonder what happened to you. I recall speaking to one of my ex's family members just after our relationship ended. The family member was concerned about my ex's motives and the kind of predicament she had gotten herself into. She even admitted telling my ex that she's making a mistake and that she should try to make things right. But, we all know that when a cheater has it set in her mind to do what she wants, nothing can stop her. That's just the nature of the beast I suppose.

64

I can't make any of you not cheat on your mates, but at least consider how your actions will affect others. Don't be a coward or subject yourself to everyone thinking the worse of you. Don't get intimately involved with people just because you want to explore your sexuality while maintaining other relationships. If you love someone, or at least care for someone, be straightforward about your desires. Don't play games or string others along until it's convenient for you to tell the truth or until a situation comes up that seriously impacts the way others think of you. Remember, you can't create a relationship built on trust and commitment when it started out based on lies, sex, and dishonesty. Perhaps the most important thing I can say to you is that you must show others the same kind of respect you want shown to you. Personally, I have a hard time respecting anyone who couldn't respect me enough to at least be honest about her intentions. In my opinion, it's an irrational, selfish, imprudent, and loathsome person who will put someone through unnecessary turmoil just to satisfy her own sexual and emotional desires.

Here are a few more things I'd like to mention on the subject of infidelity. Infidelity is about more than just sexual encounters. You violate your commitment to your mate at any point you actively engage in kissing someone else, have oral sex with someone else, or even maintain inappropriate level of restraint with someone else. By this, you allow certain boundaries with other people to be crossed just enough to make you wonder "what if?" Infidelity is also about emotional intimacy as well. You allow yourself to get so caught up with sharing your personal thoughts, desires, and daily life activities with someone other than your mate because you feel more comfortable. This can be dangerous.

Here is one final note. If you have been betrayed by someone who cheated on you, it's okay to be angry, resentful, and bitter – at first. You will have to come to a point where you stop wallowing in your own self pity and not blame yourself for someone else's actions. If you have remained faithful to this person and have been honest in your dealings with this person, you have nothing to worry about. You will feel hurt and for a while. You may even feel depressed or sad. But you must remember this. Your mate violated the basic tenets of a committed relationship, not you. Dr. Glass also states, "Life may appear to favor the deceitful partner, but in my experience, the abandoned partner often ends up with a better life than before" (Glass, p. 364).

So, after you have gotten over this situation, it's time to move on to greater things. You are now empowered with greater awareness and the knowledge that you will win in the end, not the person who betrayed your trust. It's time to look forward, channel your efforts to learning from the past, and take that information to your next relationship. However, do not let the problems with the person who betrayed you hinder you from being happy in your next relationship. Remember, you will be a much better person without that person in your life. I know I am happier and live a much more fulfilling life than I used to.

The Rules of Disengagement

It is sometimes hard to walk away from a long relationship, but it is oftentimes the best thing to do. But how do you do that? How do you walk away from someone you have been involved with for so long? What will happen from now on? Can the two of you still be friends? What will your family think? I asked myself these same questions on a number of occasions. I wondered how I was going to get by. I wondered if I would miss her. It takes a lot of courage to walk away. When it's forced upon you to leave a relationship, the decision to leave is more difficult. In one of my relationships, it was hard to step aside, but I had to. It was either that or be somewhere I didn't want to be. Throughout this whole process, I discovered there are certain standards to follow in order to end a relationship. By following the 10 Rules of Disengagement, you will be able to walk away and actually be happy.

First, keep a close eye on so-called friends and watch their interaction with your sweetheart. People who are constantly labeled as "just a friend" will usually be more than just a friend. When your suspicions are confirmed through telephone records, unusual dinner settings, insane excuses and alibis, etc, confront her and move on. Remember, once a cheater, always a cheater and you will always have doubts about her in the future. Don't give her a second opportunity to be dishonest with you. I recall having an argument with one of my exes. By her own admission, she said she would cheat if I allowed her to walk out the door without us coming to a concrete solution. By the way, if anyone says that, accept the fact that it's already in that person to be unfaithful. You may not know when it will happen, but it will. She will eventually do so and you will be left saying to yourself, "she told me so."

Second, if it is impossible to remain friends with your ex, do not maintain any form of contact with her. Doing so will more than likely cause her to have the upper hand over you and essentially send a ton of mixed signals. To continue contact makes it more difficult for you to move forward to someone much better. One of the worse things you can do is to do favors for her. If you see her name on your caller id, quickly press the "ignore" button and go on with your day. Even if she calls in the middle of the night frantic and on the verge of breakdown, hang up and go back to sleep. Let the relationship go. In my case, there is absolutely no way in a dozen hells I could, or have any desire to, remain friends with my exes. With the exception of one person, remaining friends with my exes is definitely not a good idea.

Third, do not engage in intimate activities with your ex, especially if she cheated on you. She broke her commitment to you and your relationship the moment she engaged in sexual intercourse with someone else. So, don't be intimate with her. This includes kissing, fondling each other, or any other intimate activity. If she had sex with someone else while still in a relationship with you, you do not want to risk acquiring AIDS or any other sexually transmitted disease. While the likelihood of this happening among lesbians is fairly low, it is not impossible especially if you know nothing about the person she slept with. It is possible the other person has had intercourse with someone who is infected with an STD, including AIDS. Just as there are gay men who live their lives "on the down low," women are capable of doing the same. So, if she insists that you come over to "watch TV," don't do it. She may have a different agenda and will do whatever she can to tempt you. Don't put yourself in a situation where you have to describe things later as something that "just happened." By not engaging in sexual intercourse even after her repeated advances, you still maintain some amount of leverage over her and it shows you value your body even if she doesn't value her own body. Just stick to your guns. If she wants to present herself as a garden tool, let her.

I suppose what I am about to say can be labeled *Part B* of the discussion about intimate relations with your ex. I hope that neither one of you has done what I am about to say. If so, you should be ashamed. When the relationship between you and your ex is over, please don't use any of the sexual toys that you used on each other with someone else. That means, if you have to buy a new Doc Johnson with the patented "Vacu-Lock System," do it. Cock rings, bullets, rabbits, and all the other toys that are used in the bedroom are included. I once knew a young lady who made a conscience decision to use the same dildo and harness she shared with her girlfriend on the person she decided to have an outside relationship with. This is disgusting. Please respect yourself enough and invest in new items.

Fourth, be ready to go into survival mode. Throughout the relationship, maintain a separate account of about $1,500 - $2,000 that will allow you to obtain housing and other essentials. She doesn't have to know about this account unless you choose to tell her. Sometimes you can tell when the relationship is headed downhill and there may not be a chance to fix it. In this case, you'll need a separate account. This account is separate from your emergency fund, which should only be used for emergency car repairs, hospital expense, etc. This account is also separate from your regular savings account, which should be used for short-term goals like a new television or a vacation. Having a separate account is not a sign of dishonesty, but rather is a way of protecting yourself against the unknown. No relationship is guaranteed to last forever no matter how much you claim you love the other person. Joint accounts create problems for both of you in case of a separation. Be sure to check other accounts that you may have in case of a separation. If you have any 401k accounts, IRAs, insurance policies, etc. pay careful attention to the beneficiaries of those accounts. If anything tragic should happen to you, it would make your family livid if your ex benefited from your death. Besides having your own money keeps you from worrying if your money is being used to entertain someone's mistress. I was able to save more than $3,000 in my own personal account that no one other than myself knew existed. It made my ex upset to know I had this account, but it was mine and she couldn't touch it. Now that's power.

Fifth, avoid contact with mutual friends. Doing this will minimize the risk of your ex finding out about your happiness, sadness, success, and failures from these friends. It's not your ex's business to know what happens to you once the relationship has ended. In addition, if you are having a hard time adjusting to the breakup, it may make her feel better knowing about your pain. Don't give her the satisfaction. You also want to avoid mutual friends because you don't want to put those friends in the middle of your situation, forcing them to perhaps choose sides. Nobody wants to be in this position. Then again, a mutual friend may have been one of those "she's just a friend" types that you didn't know about or didn't suspect. Mutual friends can be both assets and liabilities. They will hang out with you, give you advice, and all kinds of other stuff. When it all comes down to it, they will remain loyal to the friend they knew first. It doesn't matter that they feel you were wronged or anything like that. What matters is their long-term friendship with your sweetheart. So stay away from them for your own sake.

Sixth, avoid contact with family members. If the relationship is over, there is no need to maintain contact with Big Mama, Auntie, or anyone else in the family. If the relationship ended on bad terms, definitely DO NOT contact the family. They will not have warm, fuzzy feelings about you even if you did nothing wrong. They probably got a different side of the story so automatically you're the bad guy. In some cases, the ex's family realizes that their daughter, niece, aunt, cousin, or sister messed up and hearing from you may confirm that fact. Your ex doesn't want that to be the situation. Your ex's goal is to maintain the unbalanced scales of purity in their favor even if they are wrong. It's sometimes necessary for you to acknowledge the fact that your exes are cut from the same cloth as their family. Sometimes your exes will exhibit some of the same overall qualities as their family members. By this, I mean the family members may have a jealous nature, be mean-spirited, or only focused on their well-being. Why deal with them outside of your failed relationship with the ex anyway? I can't think of any family members of any of my exes that I would remotely want to keep in contact with.

Seventh, don't lend your ex money. She is not your responsibility. If she cheated on you, let her new girlfriend be her source of provision. If not, lending your ex will continue to create problems for you because it will only continue to tie the two of you together. This is not healthy. If there are any joint assets like bank accounts, automobile loans, leases, credit cards, etc., do what is necessary to release yourself from liability as quickly as possible. If you don't, then you risk having credit issues later. Watch out for these people very carefully. By that, I mean those exes who will keep tapping you for funds until their situation looks a little clearer and then they're gone. Some people call these types of women "gold-diggers" and you suddenly become a convenient friend. Sometimes convenience-seekers will try to fill your head with all kinds of dreamy scenarios to keep you holding on for a while longer. For example, they may say something like "I want to be with you, but I have to take care of myself first." Perhaps they want to secure more stable employment and need you around for a bit longer. Perhaps they're waiting for the right moment to bring in the so-called "friend" to help out with expenses. Whatever the reason, please keep your wallet sealed. She's on her own and you should allow her the opportunity to fail if that is what is in her destiny to do. If you've both moved on to other people, let it be.

Eighth, if possible, equally divide all tangible assets or sell them and split the profits. This includes furniture, stereos, televisions, etc. I don't see why these things shouldn't be split if they were acquired during the relationship. On the other hand, if your ex holds on to the fact that she bought everything and you know it's not true, let her be happy with her lies. If it's not worth going through what it takes to recoup your investment, let it go. Besides, you don't need to be reminded of all the hassles, disappointments, and resentment you may feel for her if you regain those things and they are in your presence. A more practical solution is to establish a partnership agreement at the beginning of the relationship. This is a binding agreement that stipulates what will happen to assets, living arrangements, finances, etc. if the parties separate. An attorney can easily set this up for you at an affordable rate or you may choose to complete a do-it-yourself tenant agreement. Office supply stores and most online legal services agencies like legalzoom.com can provide this information.

Ninth, if you were married, pawn your rings and any other expensive jewelry once the relationship is over. You can't use them again anyway or at least you shouldn't. This is another way of officially disengaging the relationship. In each of my failed relationships, it was best for me to not only get rid of all jewelry, I tossed anything that reminded me of my exes into the trash including pictures, clothing, letters, cards, and so on. It felt good tossing my exes' pictures and other items into the trash. I smiled. The only things I couldn't get rid of were the memories. But those will always stick with you. It's not easy to just be rid of them.

Tenth, at the first sign of physical abuse, get out and do not return. There is no reason to stay around and be with someone who has the audacity to raise her hand to you. Your body is not to be used as a punching bag when she gets frustrated or upset. There is no argument, financial issue, or woman in the world worth exchanging blows. The best thing to do is walk away, or if necessary, defend yourself and call the police. You both may go to jail depending on the situation, but going to jail is a lot better than subjecting yourself to someone else's unwarranted violence.

The most important rule, above all others, is to be happy. It may not feel good to lose that relationship, but it will in time. You will realize that person wasn't the person for you. You will realize your own mistakes and you'll know how to deal with these types of situations later if they should arise again. Most importantly, you will be happier without that person in your life and you will find someone else who will be much better suited for you. And for any cheating, abusive, or disrespectful exes, just remember that what goes around always comes around. I know that sounds a little cliché, but it's true. We can't expect to treat others wrong and not have some sort of consequences. We can't expect to be dishonest without being met with the same type of dishonesty. Not only is it important for you to be happy, it's important for you to recognize that it's not up to you to seek revenge. That is the worse thing you can do. Instead, let God work His magic

The Past is Our Greatest Teacher

Getting back into the dating scene can be a frightening task. Dating after a long relationship has ended can also be disastrous. The type of people you may encounter will vary on a number of levels. When my marriage ended, the people I met were very interesting for a number of reasons. A few had kids. Two were married or going through a divorce. Some were bisexual. Some were business owners or had very successful careers. I remained friends with some of them and others were just short of needing a psychiatrist. Some of these characteristics overlapped and defined the personalities of more than one person. I even had the opportunity to be friends with or date exotic dancers and in one case, an escort. Escorts, I must mention, are interesting. They are glorified customer care specialists who do what it takes to please a customer. My experience with them, however, has been nothing more than a casual, strictly platonic relationship. Throughout the whole dating ordeal, I quickly learned what it meant to simply date and what it meant to be in a relationship with someone who is not your equal. I also learned to never do it again.

When you've been in a relationship for a while, you tend to become comfortable. You know each others' habits, likes and dislikes, fears, and so on. You're able to understand each other in ways no one else can. Many of the decisions you make revolve around how it will affect your relationship. When that relationship ends, however, your comfort zone becomes a place of uncertainty. Your first thought may be "what should I do?" You may be confused, angry, hurt, and disappointed. You may feel a host of other emotions as well that make you question what happened and why things happened the way they did. Understand that it is customary to feel these emotions. It is customary to be in a strange state of mind when it comes to losing a relationship you have been so intimately involved in for a long time.

However, no matter what caused that relationship to end, it is imperative not to take the problems associated with that experience to your next

71

relationship. You could actually do more harm than good. When my last long term relationship ended, it turned out to be a very traumatic experience. On the one hand, I felt a powerful sense of relief knowing I was not with that person anymore. I was extremely happy that I no longer had to deal with someone else's insecurities, doubts, sensitivity, and lack of self esteem. I was happier about the fact that I did not spend any more of my precious time dealing with someone who I really didn't want to be with anymore, but was unsure of the best way to say good-bye.

On the other hand, I was unsure about a lot of things. Among the many questions I asked myself was "who is going to hurt me again?" "Who is going to lie to me?" "Who is going to take the things I say in confidence and attempt to use them against me?" Unfortunately, I carried all of these questions and problems I had in previous relationships to the next relationship. I found myself saying to certain people how so-and-so did this and how so-and-so caused this to happen. I refused to do certain things for people because people in previous relationships caused me to take on the mindset that I should let others protect and take care of themselves without my assistance. Perhaps I was unconsciously perpetuating those things to the point I just expected something dreadful to happen. I just wanted to be prepared and not repeat the same mistakes. I didn't want to have to look back on things and feel as if I'm experiencing déjà vu because I made the same mistakes again.

It took one person with a lot of spunk to say to me, in no uncertain terms, "damn it, I'm not those bitches so stop comparing me." I thought that her statement was a little harsh at first, but it served as a sudden reality check. It was at that point I realized I was probably causing more trouble for myself than I really needed and that I allowed ex-wives and girlfriends to keep me trapped in a past I anxiously wanted to forget. I really just wanted to turn the page and start a happier, more fulfilling chapter of my life that was not riddled with animosity and regrets.

In my quest to move forward and enjoy dating again, I learned a lot about people and my interaction with them. I learned the importance of dating and why it's imperative not to rush into a new relationship. No matter how hard you try or want it to happen, it is not possible to go from one relationship to the next and immediately find love. The person who does this realized her feelings for someone else and was intimately involved with that person long before ending their current relationship. In addition, the person who does feel she has found instant love after leaving a long term relationship is starry-eyed and has a narrow-minded perception of love and the concept of being in love.

The most important thing I learned is that it is absolutely necessary for you to first find healing before you move into a new relationship. Healing means you have come to a very critical point in your life where you are okay with the fact that your previous relationship ended and there were certain factors that perhaps you didn't realize before the relationship officially terminated. For example, maybe you didn't fully comprehend the fact that your sweetie actually wanted to control your every move until late in the relationship.

Perhaps you, like me, realized that the person you were with used to be the sweetest lollipop at the Quickie Mart with the cutest wrapper in the world. However, by the time you took the wrapper off to begin enjoying the first few licks, you began to see all the imperfections. You tasted the bitterness that often comes with such a treat. You were ultimately disappointed. The best looking and sweetest tasting lollipop in the world suddenly became one of your worse objects of delight ever. This is the moment you realize that everything that looks good and tastes good is not healthy for you. So, Big Mama's red velvet cake with the homemade icing and fresh nuts may take the top prize at any nationwide bakeoff. But you know for a fact, as you continue to do hammer curls with your fork and stuff your mouth with the moist velvet and creamy treat, three servings of Big Mama's delicious cake could lead to diabetes, high blood pressure, obesity, and so on.

This is exactly what happened to me. I was involved in relationships, one in particular, where initially my sweetie seemed to be the most perfect person in the world. I could count on her to be there for me. I could talk to her about anything under the sun and not feel ashamed or have reservations about sharing my secrets. There was no one else in the world for me at that time. Suddenly my perfect sweetheart turned into an intolerable sweet tart with the ability to influence anyone along her way of thinking. She finally became someone I could barely recognize anymore and someone whom I desperately wanted to be free of. Sometimes a change in a person's personality and overall disposition will cause you to go from being happy one minute to being sad the next. For a long time, I was happy and then sad because I was no longer content being with the same person. I found myself looking for every excuse in the world not to be home. Late nights at work, pretending to be sick, spending time with family, or just wanting to watch television were just some of the excuses in my arsenal that I used to try to maintain what was left of my sanity and to avoid as much confrontation as possible. It took a while for me not to think about certain people in my past without getting angry. This is the first step to healing.

Healing also requires you to take account of all the things that have happened in previous relationships and decipher the lessons to be learned in each of those experiences. If you were involved in a relationship where you discovered your sweetie was being dishonest, hopefully you have learned how to detect certain cues and watch out for changes in behavior, spending habits, attitude, and so forth. If you were in an abusive relationship, hopefully you have learned that your body is not to be used as a target for anyone's frustration and that you love yourself more than you love your abuser. Think about the things you have done to cause your relationships to end as well. If you were in a relationship and you were the aggressive and controlling type, hopefully you have learned to actually listen to what the other person wants and respect her desires. Perhaps you were the one who didn't want your sweetie to be around anyone but you. Hopefully you have learned that when people are in relationships, they need time away from each other to socialize, have fun, or just enjoy some peace and tranquility alone at the lake or at the movies.

When you've finally reached your healing point and you have taken into consideration the lessons you've learned by going through certain relationships, you have to be careful who you give yourself to again. Dating is like an extended interview where the objective is to find a mate who is compatible with you mentally, physically, emotionally, financially, sexually, and spiritually. You must evaluate your own personal needs and what you desire in a mate. Determine which things are most important to you. Is it important for your ideal mate to be intelligent, witty, or a good listener? Perhaps your ideal mate is one who is artistic, a good kisser, or someone who loves to dance. Perhaps your ideal mate is romantic and sensitive.

Whatever criteria you set for your ideal mate, be sure you are honest with yourself and those you encounter. Remember, it is crucial to be involved with someone who will bring you up and support you. Do not get involved with someone who will bring you down or who will find satisfaction in your possible demise. You should definitely try to stay away from people who unconsciously present themselves as being cunning and manipulative as these are the ones who use even your family as a weapon against you. These are the people who want to intentionally hurt you because they have been hurt in the past either by others or supposedly by you. They want to take advantage of you in any way possible. There are a lot of people in the world today who fit this type of description. They are mean and manipulative people and should be avoided. In the course of writing this book, I found three examples of people to be cautious of in your search for romantic happiness. They include people like the Greek goddess, Persephone, the Duke University Lacrosse team alleged rape victim, Crystal Mangum, and the Biblical character, Delilah.

There is a lot you can learn from one of the most talked about goddesses in all of Greek mythology, Persephone. The story of Persephone has been a topic of scholarly discussion for many years. She has been referred to in different contexts in Homer's *The Odyssey*, Virgil's *The Iliad*, and countless other classical works. One of the reasons Persephone's story is worthy of mentioning is that for a goddess with such youthfulness, energy, and beauty, she is also described as very mysterious and vengeful.

Greek mythology and many scholarly articles tell us that when Persephone was younger, she was picking flowers in a small garden. She struck the attention of Hades, the God of the Underworld. Allegedly, Hades kidnapped and forced Persephone to live in the underworld with him. As part of an agreement made between Hades and Zeus, Persephone's father, Persephone was allowed to spend six months of the year above ground with her mother, Demeter, and the remaining six months with Hades. This, according to scholars, is the basis for the change of the seasons.

For the most part, Persephone has been portrayed as a victim, someone who was taken against her will to spend a part of the rest of her life in darkness. However, there is evidence to suggest that Persephone willingly went to be with

Hades where she became known as the Queen of the Dead. Citing several other scholars to defend his notion that Persephone wasn't abducted, Jeffrey Kishner notes that "[people] hide themselves behind a façade of 'purity.' In Persephone we see this in the fact that she actually stays with her dark husband and...give birth to a child, Dionysos" (Kishner, p. 1). Kishner goes on to report there was never a mention of any struggle or appeal to leave Hades. Kishner finishes up his argument by stating that Persephone's "ability to move between both worlds fluidly suggests...a unique step in development. She was thoroughly aware of the depths, the soul of her being and had mastered death" (Kishner, p. 1). In other words, Persephone had free will to do what she wanted to do. No one forced her to go with, or even stay with Hades. She was well aware of what was happening and the consequences associated with her decision.

What can we learn from Persephone, the much debated goddess of the Underworld? I have learned that people will sometimes attempt to portray themselves in the most positive light possible. They will try to convince others that the decisions they've made in their lives were forced upon them and the way they carry out their day-to-day activities is because of certain people or events that have taken place in their lives. They will try to convince others that they have been harmed in some way. They will present their stories to others as if they were justified in acting in certain ways, even if their account of what happened is far from the truth and virtually void of anything that remotely resembles reality. These are actually very bitter people who want nothing more than for someone to feel sympathetic to their cause. They will say and do so many things to support their claims, while beneath the surface, they have other plans. They want people to believe what they say and coddle their wounded self esteem and pride. Stay away from this type of person because she has only two goals in life. The first is to lure you to her way of thinking with her dazzling smile and heart-wrenching life story. The other goal is to manipulate you to do what she wants you to do even if it means sacrificing your own happiness.

Persephone's story reminds me of the Duke Lacrosse Case in which Crystal Mangum accused members of the Duke University lacrosse team of rape and sodomy. Every member of the team was initially a suspect in the case and then the case revolved around three particular players on the team. Mangum claimed she was attacked while she was working as an exotic dancer at a social function off campus. The case against the lacrosse players was eventually dropped due to the alleged victim's inconsistent account of what happened and poor, malicious counsel on the part of the District Attorney, Mike Nifong. Shortly after the charges against the lacrosse players were dropped, Nifong was criticized by members of the legal community at an ethics hearing. North Carolina Attorney General, Roy Cooper, told CBS news "When you have a prosecutor who takes advantage of his enormous power and overreaches like this, then yes, it's offensive" (Gardner, p. 1). One of the reasons the Lacrosse case is so important is that Nifong never interviewed Mangum to get her side of the story until months after the case started. By his own admission, Nifong stated, "In retrospect, that would have been a good idea…all the people who had spoken to Ms. Mangum were convinced she was telling the truth" (Porteus, p.2). This is interesting because later in the case, Mangum admitted she wasn't sure if she was really raped. It's interesting to note that Mangum has had a history of accusing other men in her life of rape, kidnapping, and physical threats (Park, p. 2).

What can be learned from Mangum and Nifong? Be cautious of people who falsely accuse you of something without proof. These are the people who want you to be punished for something you never did. Sometimes they just want to be a catalyst and witness to the fact that your name and reputation are being compromised. Sometimes they are so out of touch with reality, they think the world should believe whatever they say because they showed a few tears or talked about how they feel harmed in some way. Oftentimes, people will view this type of ordeal as a game with the main objective being to ultimately destroy you or take everything of value from you. Their designated target could be your home, your finances, your wife or girlfriend, and in some cases your freedom. These people are dangerous because they really can't be trusted to do what's morally right. They will take shortcuts and attempt to create a situation in which they come out on top at any cost. Someone else's feelings are not important. Like many people in the world, all they care about is what gives them satisfaction. They want you to be their stepping stone to that end. They have no concept of what's right or wrong and they don't really care. I don't trust people like Crystal Mangum because they are more concerned with getting what they want at your expense. Stay away from this type of person.

The last type of person I would like for you to watch out for is anyone who resembles Delilah. In the Bible, Delilah, a Philistine, was married to Sampson. Sampson was strong and courageous. He was called by God to defeat the Philistines. His only weakness, however, was the loss of his long hair. Delilah was asked by the Philistines to find out the nature of Sampson's weakness. On three separate occasions, Delilah asked Sampson to tell her the source of his weakness. Sampson gave her false responses, but she acted on each one. After the third time, she gets upset and asks Sampson why he chose to make a fool of her by not answering correctly. Eventually, he responds truthfully and Delilah takes full advantage of the opportunity to subdue him. Sampson is attacked and his hair is cut off. He subsequently loses his strength.

Delilah teaches us to be careful of what you say to people and how you act toward them. Some people will try to make their way into your life because of the things you have and the things you can do for them. Some people will pretend to be your best friend and confidant, but what they're really doing is reaching into your chest of secrets to see what they can use against you. If you tell people things that you've done in your past, they may use that as leverage against you to make you do what they want you to do. Some people will take you out to a fancy restaurant and to a Broadway show and feel that because they spent $200 on you for a three hour date, you are obligated to give them your $200 million body. Delilah also teaches us that just because you are married to

76

someone, don't think they will not screw you over. Your so-called loving wife will be one of the first ones to let you down in a time of need. She will sometimes take pride in watching you suffer. This is not the type of person you should waste your time dealing with.

So, when you get back into dating again, remember to be careful with the people you choose to share your life with. Look for anything that might suggest to you that this person may not be good for you. Listen for certain cues, behavior patterns, words, and anything else that might suggest to you that the person you're considering being in a relationship with may actually be someone like Persephone, Mangum, or Delilah. Stay true to the criteria you have set for your ideal mate and don't settle for anything less. Don't rush to be in a relationship with someone just to be with someone. That's not healthy. Take your time and enjoy dating. Learn how to be friends with people before you become intimately involved with them. When you do things this way, you will be much happier.

The Cost of Liberation

In the process of writing this book, I was involved in a car accident. There were no other vehicles involved other than my red Ford F150 that I affectionately call Big Sexy. I was driving down a road that I had traveled many times before. I knew every curve, every pothole, and every major spot where a deer or unsuspecting squirrel or rabbit may dart aimlessly into the flow of traffic. Usually, there are young mothers and fathers or health-conscience elderly men or women who set out during the early morning hours on their daily walk, but not on this day. I was glad I was the lone traveler that day.

It happened at 6:45 on a Sunday morning. I was about ten miles from my comfortable bed and my watchdog Pomeranian, Leo. I was tired, but I really couldn't wait to get home. At some point, I lost control of Big Sexy. I heard a loud bang and the sound of metal crashing into itself. Before I knew it, I was spinning in circles as if I was a load of laundry on its final spin cycle. I desperately tried to stop, but it was no use. My hands were wrapped tightly around the stirring wheel and were working diligently to control it so as not to crash into a nearby immutable object. All I could see were telephone poles and a glimpse of a white vehicle that had stopped just short of my horrific ordeal to witness what was happening and perhaps offer assistance if needed. I closed my eyes briefly and hoped for the best while wishing I wasn't going through this carnival ride gone awry.

Big Sexy finally came to a stop. I opened my eyes and looked around. My first thought was, "I'm not dead" and I was very thankful. I touched my chest, my legs, and finally my temples. I looked at my hands hoping that I wouldn't see any blood. I wasn't hurt, but I was shaken up and felt the adrenaline rushing tirelessly throughout my body. I opened the door, stepped outside, and took a look at my surroundings. The smell of burnt rubber permeated the air. Skid marks had taken up about seventy-five percent of the road at various places.

I walked around to the other side only to discover that my rear right tire was completely off the rim. My rear axle appeared to be broken. My left tire and rim were slightly bent inwards. There was no body damage, however.

78

As I waited for the police and a wrecker to tow my vehicle to the dealer for repairs, I looked at my surroundings again. After all of the spinning, the relentless skidding, and desperation braking was finally over, Big Sexy made her final resting stop next to a telephone pole that was about four feet from the driver's door. An event that lasted an agonizing fifteen seconds or less could have cost me my life. God was definitely on my side. It wasn't my time to meet Him just yet.

I have never been in an accident of this magnitude before. I was scared. My life could have ended in those few seconds and my family would have been planning my funeral instead of helping me celebrate this book. I began thinking about the events that have occurred in my life over the past thirty-three years. There were some moments I felt very proud about – graduating from college and eventually earning my Master's Degree, getting past those stressful teenage years, learning how to cook without causing a three-alarm fire, and a host of other things. I have also had my share of regrets. I've been other people's lifeboat in their sea of raging trouble and have oftentimes sacrificed my own security and happiness because of it. After my last marriage, I allowed myself to be aligned with people who didn't necessarily have my best interest in mind, but it took a while for me to see it. I thought I had strong feelings for them, maybe even love for one in particular. However I was wrong. The problem was that I wanted to feel the way I did during the early years of my last serious relationship and I tried to force those feelings to reemerge in a new person. That is what made me unhappy and caused me to focus my efforts on writing.

Earlier in this book, I mentioned what it means to be liberated. When specific people and things have been permanently released from our mind, our hearts, and our soul, we are liberated. When we can mention the person's name or hear the voice of who wronged us, lied to us, or mistreated us in some way without wanting to shout the first obscenity that comes to mind, we are liberated. I once ran into one of my exes and I was shocked by my response. For a long time, I had nothing but hatred, disgust, and disdain for her. I hoped each day would be the day that she met some type of misfortune, although not a physical one that would affect her health and certainly not anything that I would personally perpetrate. But I wanted her to hurt financially, emotionally, mentally, sexually, and any other way I could possibly think of. I wanted her to know what it's like to be betrayed and misled. Each day, I hoped that someone would hurt her and make her feel the things she made me felt. Nowadays, I just regret the fact that my memory still keeps her a part of my thoughts from time to time.

The key to being liberated, however, is not missing who or what you leave behind or wishing misfortune on anyone. Instead, it is important to be able to speak on these things with indifference and in some cases, with passion and an indisputable amount of courage. This gives you the freedom to do anything you choose. If you have been liberated from a physically abusive relationship, surely you wouldn't desire to be with your abuser again and you

79

wouldn't miss being kicked or hit in any kind of way. But when you leave that relationship, you feel better. The wounds may take time to heal and you may need additional counseling, but in the end you will feel great because now your body belongs to you again. You may even find yourself in a position to mentor others and be a role model to other women.

Liberation, however, comes with a price tag. What are you willing to give up? What are you willing to do to experience the euphoria of being liberated? If your life depended on it, who would you be willing to say goodbye to? The price for liberation is high because it requires you to be an active participant in the liberation process. It also requires you to recognize and accept the fact that you have an obligation to be honest with yourself and everyone you meet. There are three important rules to remember that will aid in your liberation process.

First, take responsibility for your actions and don't make promises you can't keep. When you get that shiny Platinum plastic card from Macy's, you promise them that you will pay them every month on the 15th. When the bill comes and your minimum amount due is $300, you are quick to ask for payment arrangements. You created the debt, now pay it. In relationships, don't promise someone you will be honest and faithful for a zillion years when down the line, you are making excuses for your whereabouts and using friends to help you with your alibis. You have instantly created an environment in which you can't be trusted. If you can't be trusted, no one in their right mind is going to want to be with you. What is the purpose of maintaining the relationship with you in the first place? If you're the type who finds it cool to have several relationships at the same time, don't be surprised when you end up with someone who doesn't take too kindly to being the other woman. Take responsibility for your actions and be honest with everyone you meet.

Second, know that concession is never an option. When you have conceded to someone else's insecurities, doubts, or negativity, you are allowing her to control everything you do. Suddenly your dreams and aspirations become nothing more than a passing thought. If you've ever seen the Peachtree Road Race, the Boston Marathon, or any other type of race like these, you see how tired the runners are. They're sweating profusely, some pass out before the race is over, and others continue by shear instinct alone. It's this last group of people who refuse to quit. They are exhausted, but their goal is to finish the race far. This type of determination far exceeds the fatigue they experience. In life, some of us dream of owning our own business. We fight through the long hours of researching the industry and marketing. We sacrifice our time and money just to be the boss. Despite the challenges and pitfalls, you must never quit. Throughout the course of your journey, if someone is put in your path, ask her for guidance or tell her to leave. To fully achieve your goals, you must be focused. When someone tries to take that focus from you, it's because they're either jealous of you or they want you to give up.

Finally, the most important thing to remember is that you have an obligation to God to be and do what He has called you to do. He doesn't owe you anything. So while it only took you an hour to accumulate over $2,000 in debt at Macy's, don't expect God to show up and pay your bill with a winning quick pick lotto ticket or a surprise check in the mail. We all have the freedom to do the things we want to do. If we choose to stay in unhealthy relationships, it's by choice. If we keep running back to the things and people that are causing us stress and pain in our bodies, it's by choice. God isn't going to step in at just the right moment to keep us from making some choices in life. We have to learn from our mistakes. Instead, God has called us to do great things and to live in a spirit of faith, not fear. We owe Him that. If He can give us His only son for all of our bad choices in life, what are you willing to do for Him?

In summary, you must pay for liberation. This is done by taking responsibility for your actions, facing each of life's challenges head on without giving in to fear, and knowing that what God has for you is meant for you. So if you're in a relationship that is causing you pain or grief, leave. If someone is constantly lying to you, causing you to doubt yourself or your abilities, leave. If your dream is to write a bestselling book and be a part of Oprah's Book Club, write it. If you want to free your mind of all the negativity and heartache that your previous relationships put you through, determine what makes you happy and go for it.

I paid dearly for liberation. I was in relationships that I should never have been involved with in the first place. I was involved with people I wasn't happy with anymore. I experienced pain in my body because I was afraid of what was ahead of me. I took all of the feelings and emotions I had about certain things and bottled them up so tightly that I didn't know how to talk to people anymore. Now, I accept the fact that those things were caused by staying in those relationships and staying in a place where I didn't belong anymore. I failed to see how it was past time for me to move on and achieve my own personal greatness.

I don't miss any of the people from my past. I don't have a desire to be with them anymore, nor do I have a desire to find out how they're doing. My main concern is what's best for me. When you reach a point in your life when things are not going so well or you find you can't trust the people you once trusted, it takes a lot out of you. You are haunted by images of things that happened or things that were said. If you can turn these things into a positive, you are well on your way to liberation. For example, so what if she cheated on you or lied to you about something. Once you get over the anger, be happy about it. That person wasn't meant for you anyway. So what if your friends turn their back on you when you really need them. That just shows you who your real friends are and who you can really depend on. You have to go through a lot just to get to the very best and God only wants the very best for you. Again, what are you willing to do?

Confessions

When I began writing this book, I was very upset. I was angry at all of the people who made promises and then in a heartbeat, broke them all without regard to my feelings or how their actions would affect our relationship. I was angry that the things I wanted most in life seemed light years away and that my dreams were slowly slipping away from me. I was angry that my efforts to help people in need turned out to be mistakes and that I should have let them fall victim to circumstance and consequences. My genuine desire to help people got in the way of more deliberate thought and reservation.

I was even mad at God. I recall challenging God by demanding Him to show up in my life at specific times and places and do exactly what I wanted Him to do. I challenged God to somehow deliver me from the choices I made. I was going through so much. I came close to eviction. I had bills that I could not pay. My friends couldn't understand why I didn't want to hang out or talk on the phone. Every relationship I became involved in was haunted by the problems I carried over from previous relationships, one in particular. I said to God, why are you doing this to me? Have I done something wrong? What am I being punished for? Why am I being treated as the bad guy? I figured even God was against me despite what my years of faith have taught me.

Before long, I realized that God was not the issue. God was not upset with me or attempting to punish me. He was trying to talk to me and I wasn't listening. He was trying to tell me to let go of certain people and I was still holding on to people and things that had long outlived their expiration date. When God tried to speak to me, I was too busy trying to figure things out on my own.

Most of all, I was angry at certain people in my life for all the things they put me through. I found myself thinking of the country music group Rascal Flatts and their hit song, *"My Wish."* In that song, they proclaim, "my wish for you is that this life becomes all that you want it to…your dreams stay big, your worries stay small…." I couldn't bring myself to wish them well at all. For a while, I recall wishing bad things would happen to them, nothing of a

82

physical nature of course. My heart is not such to wish physical pain on anyone. I wanted them to feel emotional pain so severe that it crippled their efforts to concentrate on even the smallest tasks. I wanted someone to break their heart so badly, they would spend hours crying about it and asking themselves, "why me?" I wanted them to be full of so much anger, that even praying would not bring them peace. I wanted them to ask if God was upset with them and for them to hear, without reservation or doubt, the answer, "yes."

It took going through a bad relationship and turmoil to realize that I was holding myself back. I got in the way of my own peace and tranquility and didn't realize that I had to go through those things in order to become a better person. I had to present myself to God in the most humble way in order to be healed. I had to come to a point in my life where I thought all hope was lost. For a short time, it felt that way, but then something happened.

One day, I was driving along and I heard the song, *"I Won't Complain."* There are people in my life who have come close to losing everything. I have friends who are sick and are on the verge of giving up. I have friends in my life who have been diagnosed with serious illnesses like cancer or diabetes. Some of them are going through things that only they and God can understand. And here I was complaining when I never missed a meal. I was never homeless. I had money in the bank and lots of it. Most importantly, I had one or two close friends I could really depend on. I stopped Big Sexy and had a long cry. After that, my situation started to change drastically. I am more focused on life and the people I choose to share this life with me. It suddenly occurred to me that I was feeling sorry for myself rather than being thankful that I'm no longer the same person I used to be and that I no longer associate myself with people who called themselves my trusted friends or intimate lovers and then turned their back on me.

One of the things I've learned from this whole experience is the power of a bitter person and the threat she poses. I've learned that a bitter person is perhaps one of the most dangerous people in the world. Bitter people will always try to harm you. They find strength and satisfaction knowing that you may be struggling, depressed, hurt, sad, weary, and in some cases completely destitute. Gaining revenge is their ultimate motivation because they feel you hurt them or mistreated them in some way. Whether or not that hurt is real does not matter in the grand scheme of things. If that hurt is a part of a bitter person's reality, it becomes an irrefutable fact that you inflicted not only emotional pain, but physical pain as well. In their eyes, these are the reasons that you must be punished. This "eye for an eye" tactic is one employed by people all the time. It doesn't mean it's the right thing to do, but for some people, it is the safest way out and the best way to save face.

Bitter people will present themselves as victims and try to persuade others that they are innocent and need protection. Bitter people will try to do to you what others have done to them in the past. If they were abused, neglected, or mistreated in previous relationships or by their parents and other family members, they will sometimes inflict that same treatment on the ones they hold dear now. If they feel they have given 100% to you and do not receive that in return, according to their standards, they are justified in taking things into their own hands and creating havoc in order to make themselves feel better. Sometimes bitter people will go as far as to lie to you and about you in any way possible to destroy your character and negatively impact your way of life. What this all adds up to is a bunch of B.S.

At some point, I was very bitter as well. I hated someone with a passion so deep, it made my heart heavy. All I wanted to do is get even and bring myself the satisfaction of knowing I had the last say in things. I was angry for a long time. I allowed this person to take my joy and peace. After months of reflection, I am no longer in that space and I am definitely a better person now. I've had to rely on not just my friends to help me through certain situations, but I had to renew the greatest relationship of all – my relationship with God.

One of my favorite books in the Bible, Romans, more specifically, Romans 12, helped me realize that there is much more out there for me. It takes changing your mindset first in order to change your situation. It takes a total transformation of your way of thinking in order to change your life. When you begin to change your mindset, all things will be restored in your life. But, here is the tricky part. You will not receive the old things that you lost. You will have a new kind of joy and happiness. You will experience increase in your life. So, let other people keep what they have taken from you in the past. Let others laugh at you if it makes them feel good. Let them take the house, the car, and any other material possession if they feel so inclined to do so. Let them take that part of you that had been trapped for so long and keep it as a souvenir if it makes them feel good. When you're in a different mindset, you get different results and a much more positive outcome.

As for me, the people and things that I let go made me stronger. I'm happier. I'm not stressed. I'm successful despite the challenges. This book is just one small proof of that. As far as material possessions are concerned, yes I was upset about not being able to maintain some of the things of the past. But wow, football is so much better on a 73-inch HDTV with surround sound, 1080p resolution, and a BOSE surround system. Did I mention it's a flat screen and not some bulky RPTV that takes up a ton of space? Material things, however, are not as important as what some people make them out to be. They fade, lose their value, their attractiveness, ingenuity, and so on. The one thing that should be most important is a person's character. This is the one thing that truly shapes a person and how they live their life.

Sometimes life deals us a hand that no matter what, we must either ante up or fold. In relationships, we are expected to make certain sacrifices. We are asked to give ourselves to the other person completely, but sometimes we give too much. Sometimes we give so much of ourselves, that we lose our identity and our own self worth in the process. I held my true feelings inside for so long because I was afraid of the consequences of having an adult conversation to discuss those feelings. I was so unhappy, but not wise enough or sure enough to walk away. I was ready to call it quits, but I wasn't strong enough to lay down my fears and take the first step. I was like a toddler still holding on to Mama's hand so I wouldn't have to go to my first day of school, afraid that I wouldn't make new friends or fit in with the others.

I'm glad things happened as they did. I'm glad that I didn't have to fold when I was dealt what seamed like a losing hand. I'm glad those former relationships and friends are out of my life. Perhaps my life would have been different had I laid down my hands and given up. But I do not operate in that level of fear, anxiety, and anger anymore. So, when you are dealt the "right" hand, you will know it. It will be impossible for you to keep a steady, poker face. You will be excited and ready to experience anything. You will smile more. You will brazenly walk down the street and people will feel the energy that's coming from you. There will be a remarkable amount of confidence in everything you do and everything you say. People will look to you for guidance and will lean on you because of your strength and good character. You will have no fear. People will gaze upon you and wonder what is wrong with you. They will ask if you are drunk or stark mad. They will see the level of poise, tenacity, and enthusiasm you have for life. When this happens to you, and it will, brace yourself for what is yet to come. The world will have to stop and let you pass by first. You will be changed. You will be a new person. You will be liberated!

The Beginning…..

85

Reflections

I.M.

To: 000.565.6316
From: 000.767.8112
Thank You for all you've done for me.
I'm glad to have you by my side.
What a friend indeed.
TTYL, my friend for life.

POSSIBILITIES

It's impossible to love
When you don't get it in return
It's impossible to share
When what you share is used against you.
It's impossible to be committed to one person
When that person is not completely committed to you.
While love is an impossible thing to fully comprehend
All things are possible with God, your one true friend.

LIED

We talked about love and being happily ever after,
But you lied and it all started the moment you met her.
We talked about honesty and standing by each other strong,
But you lied and now my trust in you is completely gone.
You said "I do," "I will," and you will commit only to me,
But you lied and instead you chose a path of infidelity.
You said she's just a friend and there's nothing else to it,
But you lied over and over; I guess she made you do it.
How many other friends have you brought into our bed,
And how many of them have you lied to me about instead?
Nonetheless, I wish you happiness and much success, too.
No, you don't deserve that, so I guess I just lied to you.

33 HOURS

I sat there alone in a 15 by 20 foot concrete holding cell.
Scared and nervous, I was going through a living hell.
Without any shoes and an old, dingy blanket to cover me,
I desperately wished to be home in the arms of my family.
I watched people walk quickly past the thick window pane
And wondered what was their story, what was their pain.
I carefully studied my surroundings and found them inept.
I looked at the floor beneath me. Had it ever been swept?
There were no beds, only an uncomfortable wooden bench.
From across the room, I could smell the terrible stench
Of previous guests both men and women and juveniles.
There are no happy endings here, no real reasons to smile.
I watched people walk quickly past the thick window pane
And wondered what was their story, what was their pain.
I heard the thick metal doors open and then close again.
On my left and on my right, a new inmate was coming in.
I lost all sense of time. I couldn't tell the night from day.
All that comforted me was sleep and my ability to pray
That I would be out soon and this would all be behind me,
A tragic page in my past and nothing more than a memory.
I watched people walk quickly past the thick window pane
And wondered what was their story, what was their pain.
I sometimes paced across the floor to gather my thoughts.
I felt I had reached rock bottom and all my hope was lost.
Goliath found another way to show her senseless powers.
As I sat there deprived of my freedom for a full 33 hours.
I watched people walk quickly past the thick window pane
And wondered what was their story, what was their pain.
My story was one filled with hurt, anger, and deception.
My antagonist, a Goliath who tried to dispel my perception.
My eyes didn't deceive me and my heart tried to warn me,
But Goliath was stronger; her main goal was to burn me.
I prayed for peace and I prayed for a forgiving heart,
But I was too angry to know where my heart could start.
I watched people walk quickly past the thick window pane
And wondered what was their story, what was their pain.
I gazed at the walls and the ceiling, both riddled with words
Indicative of hate and anger, and then a calm voice I heard
Saying to me, "do not worry; your blessings will be many.
Be at peace, and I shall fight the battle with your enemy."
I watched people walk quickly past the thick window pane
And wondered what was their story, what was their pain.
I kept watching people walk quickly past the window pane
And I was thankful for my challenges and I will love again.

THE CONFRONTATION OF MANKIND

Why look strangely whenever I'm in your presence?
Am I not your sister and your brother, too?
Are my looks displeasing to your several senses
Or does my smile not seem bright enough to you?
Is it my hair, my eyes, or the color of my skin?
Why does your conversation end when I walk in the room?
Am I not your kin, your equal, your spiritual twin?
By asking, am I setting myself up for certain doom?
Your eyes speak disgust, but your silence speaks louder.
Would it have been better had I not drawn my first breath?
Am I not loved by you, does this make your father prouder?
To be killed by hatred daily, though not a physical death,
Is something I've experienced throughout my humble existence.
While your words and your actions attempt to subdue my body,
My spirit is far greater than you and your intolerance.
Am I not a child of God? That's what you want me to see.
Instead, I am the epitome of strength, power, style, and grace.
I am love and power personified, look at my face.

MY WOMAN

Her love's as constant as the northern star
She loves, despite my idiosyncrasy
She loves, whether we're near or far apart
No matter when, her love's in sync with me
My woman loves unconditionally
Her sweet love for me can never be marred
Her heart is as pure as fresh morning dew
She lends her heart so mine may be made whole
Whether I laugh or cry, she feels it, too
When I'm feeling lost, it's me her voice consoles
My woman comforts me, body and soul
For my sake, there's nothing she would not do
She's my sweet lady, the love of my life
Without her by my side, I'd surely die

Acknowledgments and Announcements

Thank you God for allowing me to complete this work. Thank you for the challenges and the obstacles that have led me to this point. Thank you for giving me the strength to face all of those challenges head on.

To my mother and best friend, thank you for all of your love, guidance, and support throughout the years. I just want to let you know that I was listening.

To my Granny, I love you and I miss you so much. I will always remember those small, quarter-sized pancakes and grits you made for breakfast every day and those hours you spent putting little bows in my hair on Sunday afternoon. And yes, your "Toot" is doing well. I hope you're proud of the person I have become.

To my brother, Will, you know I love you big head. You're a little stubborn sometimes, but that's just in our genes. You're no longer my little brother, but rather a husband and a father. Good luck to you in everything you do.

To "Sonny Boy," thanks for everything. I love you. You've always been there for me and I appreciate you.

Thank you Angie and Troy for being great friends. After 20 years of friendship, you're still knuckleheads. I wouldn't trade either of you for the world.

To Tammy P., Tammy R., Annise M., Charlene W., Ty M., and Germaine M., you ladies are great. Good friends are hard to find. I'm so glad I found all of you throughout my journey. You've listened to me and have been patient with me throughout all of my little struggles in life. Drinks are on me.

To the ladies in my past, you tried hard to hurt me, destroy me, and bring me to my ultimate breaking point. You've lied to me and about me. However, I am much stronger, wiser, and so much happier without any of you in my life. Life is a circle and the Universe will always respond in kind to what you put forth.

Special thanks to my pastor, ministers, and the entire church family at The Vision Church in Atlanta. "From Vision to Victory," has been a powerful message in my life since I began attending TVC in 2005. I thank you and I appreciate you. Our community is much better because of you.

I would like to recognize all of the men and women in the armed services. You face a different challenge every day. You put your lives on the line each day for all of us. There are not enough words to thank you for your hard work and dedication. On behalf of every American citizen, thank you and God bless you.

Notes

Amaechi Says '95 Percent' of Feedback is Positive. Associated Press. May 5, 2007. Retrieved June 20, 2007 from http://sports.espn.go.com/nba/news/story?id=2861621

Barondess, Mark A. What Were You Thinking. Phoenix Press. Beverly Hills. 2005.

Boortz, Neal. Somebody's Gotta Say It. HarperCollins, New York. 2007.

Boykin, Keith. Black Gay Athletes: Homosexuality and Homoerotism in Black Sports. KeithBoykin.com. 2003.

Fred Phelps and the Westboro Baptist Church: In Their Own Words. The Anti-Defamation League. June 21, 2006. Retrieved March 22, 2007 from http://www.adl.org.

Gardner, Kelly. Editor. Duke Case a Tragedy, Cooper Tells '60 Minutes.' Retrieved June 20, 2007 from http://www.wral.com/news/local/story/1274096/.

Glass, Shirley. Not "Just Friends." The Free Press. New York. 2003.

Hunter, J. Paul. The Norton Introduction to Poetry. Peter Simon, Ed. W.W. Norton & Company, Inc. New York. 1999.

Johnson, Ramone. About Gay Life. Retrieved February 15, 2007 from http://gaylife.about.com/od/index/p/billcondon.htm

Kishner, Jeffrey. Lunar Tunes Astrology: Persephone was not abducted into the Underworld. Retrieved May 10, 2007 from http://jeffreykishner.com/lunartunes/2006/09/persephone-was-not-abducted-into.html.

Loughlin, Sean. Santorum Under Fire for Comments on Homosexuality. April 23, 2003. Retrieved from CNN.com on January 25, 2007.

Means, Marianne. New Thinking on Gays in the Military. Seattlepi.com. June 20, 2007. Retrieved June 26, 2007 from http://seattlepi.nwsource.com/opinion/320571_means21.html.

Park, Michael. Crystal Gail Mangum: Profile of the Duke Rape Accuser. Retrieved June 22, 2007 from http://www.foxnews.com/story/0,2933,265374,00.html.

Porteus, Liza. Nifong Apologizes for Missteps in Duke Lacrosse 'Rape' Case, Resigns as Durham DA. Retrieved June 22, 2007 from http://foxnews.com/story/0,2933,282874,00.html.
Raskin, Richard. The 'Deprogramming' of Stephanie Reithmiller. MS. Magazine. Retrieved February 15, 2007 from http://bernie.cncfamily.com/acm/rieth1.htm. 1982.

Schnall, Maxine. What Doesn't Kill You Makes You Stronger: Turning Bad Breaks Into Blessings. Perseus Publishing. 2002.

Simpson, Alan K. Bigotry That Hurts Our Military. The Washingtonpost.com. March 14, 2007. p.A15. Retrieved May 1, 2007 from http://www.washingtonpost.com/wp-dyn/content/article/2007/03/13/AR2007031301507.html

Tessina, Tina. Gay Relationships. Jeremy P. Tarcher, Inc. Los Angeles. 1989.

About the Author

Sharon D. Smith is a native and lifelong resident of Georgia. She currently resides in the Roswell area, which is about twenty miles north of Downtown Atlanta. Her family members, most of whom reside in the Decatur and Madison areas, are also natives of Georgia. In addition to being an author and publisher, Sharon is also a certified personal trainer with a national health club. In the past three years, Sharon has been a business owner in the financial services industry and has worked in the wholesale and retail end of adult entertainment. She enjoys reading and writing poetry, golf, chess, basketball, football, Lifetime TV, and of course, listening to country music.

Sharon completed her undergraduate studies at Georgia State University in 2002 where she earned a Bachelor of Arts Degree in English. She went on to earn a Master of Arts Degree in Organizational Management from the University of Phoenix in 2005. Sharon has plans to attend law school in 2008. After graduation, she hopes to open her own law firm where she may practice in the field of Family Law, Corporate Law, or Sports and Entertainment Law. Just for fun, she hopes to open her own health club.